Is God Listening?

SECRETS THAT TURN TALKING TO GOD INTO WALKING WITH GOD

RICK SHELTON

Tulsa, OK

21 20 19 18   10 9 8 7 6 5 4 3 2 1

Is God Listening?
Secrets That Turn Talking to God
Into Walking with God
ISBN: 978-1-68031-196-9

Published by Harrison House Publishers
Tulsa, Oklahoma 74145
www.harrisonhouse.com

I dedicate this book to my lovely wife, Donna, who has been my partner in this wonderful pursuit of God for forty-four years; to my mom and dad, Esther and Woody, who have exemplified this beautiful life of prayer; and to all the great men and women of prayer who have paved the way for me to enjoy the glorious secrets of the *secret place*.

Endorsements

Rick's teaching is filled with powerful insights about what prayer really is and how to develop a fulfilling prayer life that really makes a difference. Jesus died to give us relationship with God—not religion—and this book provides biblical direction to help you experience real intimacy with Him.

-**Joyce Meyer**, Bible teacher and bestselling author
St. Louis, Missouri

Pastor Rick Shelton has been my dear friend for more than 20 years. He is a trusted and faithful leader. *Is God Listening?* will open your eyes to a whole new world that is available to every believer. It will inspire you to press in to a deeper walk with God and develop intimacy with Him through prayer. I highly recommend this book to everyone.

-**Dr. Rodney Howard-Browne**, Revival Ministries International ,
Tampa, Florida

Author of *Solving Your Money Problems,* Rick Shelton has **truly** done it again. Over the years I've been inspired by his leadership abilities that built one of the first mega churches in America. In his new book, *Is God Listening?* he's uncovered **13 hidden secrets** to a more powerful prayer life. Finally, we can all stop feeling guilty, because just increasing our prayer time will not create a closer relationship with God. Instead, Pastor Rick explains how first developing a closer relationship with God will automatically explode our prayer life and lead to amazing results.

-**David Crank**, Senior Pastor, FaithChurch.com , Sunset Hills, MO

The disciples' request "teach us to pray" resonates in every generation. The disciples lived in a religious world but didn't want to pray as the religious leaders did. They wanted to pray like Jesus. We, too, want to pray, but praying so easily becomes a task to be completed, like an item on a job list to be ticked.

Jesus responded to the disciples' appeal with a prayer that replicates his life; rooted in relationship, rich in theology, and replete with practical application. Rick Shelton's book, *Is God Listening?* is similar with its emphasis on our relational connection with the Maker of all things. Its uplifting tone, its consistency with scripture, and its practical insights which, like all things profound, are so simple.

I am sure that *Is God Listening?* will look great in your library. It is, however, not a book written for a shelf. It is a book to read, re-read, and pass on to anyone with a "teach me to pray" in his or her heart.

-**Timothy W Jack**, national leader in the Apostolic Church, United Kingdom

This book is a vault of prayer secrets. They're secret not because God has hidden them from us, but because people are unaware of them or the principles that prayer operates in. Rick Shelton and his wife, Donna, are not only anointed vessels for this final age, but both are experienced prayer warriors, having spent time in the throne room of the Almighty, standing in the gap, and interceding for family, friends, and members of the church they pastored. A man with this experience is never at the mercy of someone who just holds a theory. The prayer codes that are released in Rick Shelton's' book, *Is God Listening?* he has proven. Now you hold in your hand a manual of God's Word and the experiences of a man of God that you can glean from. Great lessons can be learned from those who have lived the lesson and now teach others. You will learn life changing insight, but most of all when you put into practice and act upon the instructions in this book, your talk will turn into a walk! Enjoy the Blessings!

-**Perry Stone, Jr.**, found/director, Voice of Evangelism, OCI & ISOW, Cleveland, Tennessee

Rick Shelton has had a powerful impact on my life in so many ways. He is a gift to the body of Christ worldwide. *Is God listening?* is an amazing book everyone needs to get his or her hands on. It will help you go further in your journey with God.

-**Boyd Ratnaraja**, Elim, New Zealand

As I read the pages of the manuscript for *Is God Listening?* I realized that I needed to allow what I was reading to soak into my spirit. *Is God Listening?* is not just another book about prayer, but a revelation of prayer from one of God's generals. Rick Shelton has crafted a masterpiece for those who struggle with prayer as well as those who are seasoned in prayer. Without a doubt this book will lead its readers to a greater God encounter.

-**Paul Owens**, lead pastor, Fresh Start Church, Peoria, AZ

I found myself encouraged as I turned every page. *Is God Listening?* made me want to pray rather than making me feel as though I must pray. Every Christian, whether a prayer warrior or one who prays little, will find themselves wanting and anxious to start praying in a way they never may have experienced.

-**Pat Bradley**, founder, Crisis Aid International, St. Louis, MO

This book is an absolute *must-read* for every believer wanting a healthy happy prayer life! It's full of brilliant practical insights and an abundance of spiritual truths. It will fuel your passion for prayer and help you deal with those things that have robbed you of the intimacy and delight you long for. I guarantee it will leave you wanting to experience more of Gods secret place than ever before.

-**Dave Doery**, lead pastor, Bridge Church, Melbourne, Australia

Rick Shelton, my lifetime friend, is a man of prayer. I have many memories of wonderful times of prayer with him. Rick knows and hears from God, and he is quick to take action on what he hears. After reading this book, I can now understand the secrets that make his prayer life so powerful.

-**Jack Harris**, president, Global Messenger Service, Fenton, Missouri

I consider it a privilege and honor in endorsing this book on how to have a practical prayer life from the pen of one of my good friends, Pastor Rick Shelton. I've known him for the past 30 + years as a man who has a great vision for global evangelism along with a passion for teaching people how to pray. His understanding of God and walking with Him are clearly visible in his writing. The problem with many sincere people of God is a guilt gripped life, having a wrong understanding of their father. Pastor Rick really drives that guilt away by showing the right side of our heavenly father. This is one of the best books I have come across in a long time. It is my sincere prayer that this book may be available in Hindi (to the people whom I minister) and in Tamil (to my people whose mother tongue is mine). May the Lord use this man of God whom He has chosen to be a blessing for the universal church!

-**D. Augustine Jebakumar**, general secretary, Gospel Echoing Missionary Society (GEMS), Bihar, India

I love this book; just reading it lifted my spirit. How I would have loved to have had the insights Pastor Rick writes many years ago when as a new Pastor I was torn between excitement at the possibilities, yet struggling with guilt that I was not praying as I should. I am grateful to know that I am not alone and that others also have struggled with prayer, but our journey is to also help others along the way. The ministry of Pastor Rick Shelton has greatly impacted our church and the Elim Churches of New Zealand. He has walked the journey of a local church leader and brings insight and wisdom that encourages and builds up Pastors, churches, and the everyday Christian.

-**Luke Brough**, senior minister, Elim Christian Centre , Auckland, New Zealand

Contents

INTRODUCTION

My Journey

When I was nineteen years old, I was like most Christians who desire to draw closer to God. I had spent my life up to that point as a Christian who resorted to prayer only when I had a problem or was in a jam. My most frequent prayer was *"Help!"* I knew that spending time with God in prayer was vital to a healthy spiritual life, but I just didn't know how to pray.

I experienced nothing but frustration and disappointment as I tried to build a prayer life. I would begin my prayer time in the morning only to run out of something to say within a few minutes. I thought, *This is hopeless. I'll never be a person who loves spending time in prayer every day!* I felt totally unspiritual and my attempts to pray always left me feeling condemned. I assumed something had to be wrong with me.

Perhaps your experience is similar to mine. You want to pray, but you don't know how. If so, let me assure you that there's nothing wrong with you. I didn't realize it at the time, but there was nothing wrong with me either. The truth is, every one of us needs someone who knows how to pray to teach us to pray.

I've known people who had great prayer lives, but they never shared what they knew with anyone else. I had no one to teach me, but I was determined to learn how to pray. So I began to try different things. The first day I found a quiet place and set my watch for one hour. I thought this must be the designated amount of time for prayer because Jesus said to the disciples, "Could you not watch with me one hour while I pray?"

I began by praising and thanking God for everything that came to my mind. Then I took out my list and proceeded to ask Him for everything I needed. Then I prayed for my family, the city, the nation,

1

and all the missionaries of the world. When I finished, I looked at my watch, thinking that surely an hour had passed. When I saw the time, I was devastated that it had only been five minutes!

Day after day, I did this with the same results. Each day I was exhausted and frustrated after only a few minutes of prayer, but the longing in my heart wouldn't let me give up. I kept coming back every day, adding new things to my prayer list until I was finally able to find something to say for one hour. I must admit I was impressed with myself for that accomplishment, but it didn't change the fact that something was still missing. I made my one-hour goal, but it didn't feel like I thought it would. I still didn't seem to get anything out of my time with God.

One day while listening to a sermon from a great man of prayer, I thought for sure I would find the piece I was missing. The preacher said the key is tithing your time in prayer. In other words, he was saying I would need to spend ten percent of each day with God in prayer. I quickly calculated this, and it came out to be two hours and forty minutes each day! To be honest, after struggling so hard to make it to one hour in prayer, I was angry at this idea and thought, *I'll never be a praying Christian.* Actually, I quit praying altogether for a while.

Then I discovered some of the classic books on prayer by men like A.W. Tozer, Andrew Murray, Oswald Chambers, and others. As I read these books, I noticed something very different about the prayer lives of these men. *They focused on their relationship with God rather than rules and the amount of time they spent in prayer.* As I learned from these great men, I realized I had been approaching prayer all wrong. I had it all backwards. My whole focus was on me and about me and about praying a certain amount of time, instead of simply coming into the presence of God and talking to Him because I loved and believed in Him with all my heart.

This discovery began a whole new journey for me. I laid aside my watch and set out to simply know God and draw closer to Him. This changed everything! I entered a whole new world of enjoying God's presence and basking in His love for me while pouring my love on Him. Yes, I still asked God for things and prayed for the needy people of the world, but the requests were born out of spending time with God and hearing His heart.

Over time, there were many days that I didn't want my prayer time to end. My heart was filled with joy, and I simply didn't want to leave His presence. Responsibilities called, but the time I had committed to prayer strengthened and energized me and made me ready to face whatever came that day. More than forty years have passed since then and my life of prayer has grown sweeter and richer as the years have gone by.

In describing my formerly dry, unfulfilling life of prayer, perhaps it touches some of your own desires and struggles. Like me, you may want to pray but either you don't know how or haven't yet understood the beauty of this blessed activity. Maybe you've been praying out of obligation, or maybe you run out of things to say after a few minutes. Or, most importantly, maybe you've never yet experienced a time of prayer so wonderful it creates a longing for more.

That's why you won't find me telling you in this book that you ought to pray. You already know that! What you will find as you read are the secrets I've learned along the way. Jesus called prayer the *secret place.*" And I have found there are secrets to the secret place! People miss the beauty of prayer because they don't understand the secrets.

My goal is to show you how to walk with Jesus throughout the day and remove the obstacles that keep people like you and me from a simple, loving relationship with God in prayer. Then, when it comes time to enter the prayer room, you will find praying is so much more than a time slot in the morning. As you discover that praying is a beautiful, enjoyable experience, you will no longer struggle to be consistent. It becomes an overflow from living in the presence of God twenty-four hours a day with the confidence that He isn't just hearing words being said. He is truly listening and enjoying the time we set aside for Him. It is my hope that the truths God taught me will also teach you to enjoy a rich, rewarding prayer life in communion with the heart of the Father.

My Prayer for You

Dear heavenly Father, please open our eyes and hearts to recognize and understand Your unfailing love for us. Cause us to realize that no matter how many times we have fallen, You still desire to be with us, enjoying daily, sweet fellowship. Remove the condemnation and shame that the enemy continually tries to put on us to discourage all our efforts to draw closer to You.

Let your loving conviction lead to forgiveness and a clean heart. Grant us a spirit of wisdom and revelation in the knowledge of Jesus Christ that we may come to know the hope of Your calling, the glorious inheritance that is ours and the power that is available to us through Christ in prayer. Make us to know that our worthiness to enter the secret place is not based on our own goodness, but the goodness and righteousness of our Lord and Savior, Jesus Christ. Grant us a spirit of prayer that will grow stronger and sweeter with each passing day and may Your Spirit draw us closer to You through each page of this book.

In Jesus name I pray. Amen.

Your prayer partner,

Rick Shelton

The Throne Room

Out of the midst of shimmering light,

Rainbow colors and radiant white;
Pulsing, throbbing, with life and love.
I sense a Presence in the center thereof,
Beckoning me, calling me, drawing me,
Come!

Donna Shelton
© 1995

Is God Listening?

It's a Heart Thing

Prayer is the most wonderful adventure on which you will ever embark. In the secret place of prayer, you will find forgiveness for all your failures and shortcomings and love that offers you a fresh start everyday. You will find friendship and fellowship that far surpasses any human relationship. You will hear the voice of God leading you and bringing the words of scriptures alive. You will find comfort when you're hurting, faith when you're challenged, peace when you're in the midst of a storm, and joy when you're discouraged. In the secret place of prayer, you will find power to intercede for your loved ones, boldness to petition God for your own needs, and the power of God to shape you into the person He designed you to be. Prayer is the greatest and most rewarding activity you could ever engage in, and it's how God conducts all His business on earth.

Yet, the question is, if prayer is so wonderful, why do we struggle with it so much? The answer is simple. We will never enter the secret place of prayer with our head leading the way because prayer is an activity of the heart. Prayer is entering into a loving relationship with the Creator of the Universe—not a performance before Him.

Psalm 91:1 tells us, "He who dwells in the secret place of the Most High shall abide under the shadow of the Almighty." What a great promise! We all thrill at the thought of abiding under the shadow of the Almighty God. The word *shadow* means shade and defense. In other words, God will be our shade, and He will defend us. When the children of Israel journeyed through the wilderness, God placed a cloud over them every day to protect them from the heat. At night the cloud became a fire to light their way in the dark. As long as they followed God through the cloud and the fire, they were protected from the adverse elements and given light to show the path ahead.

As we abide under the shadow of the Almighty, we also will find everything we need. God will be our protection, our provision, and a light to show us the way as we navigate through life. Notice, God doesn't provide these things for us, He *is* the provision we need. Yet we abide under His shadow only as we dwell in the secret place of the Most High.

If we're honest with ourselves, how many of us actually live in the experience of the promises of Psalm 91? It's important to understand that for every promise in the Bible, there is something we must do. If we don't meet the prerequisite of God's promise to us, the promise will be nullified. The condition to the promises of Psalm 91 is to dwell in the secret place of the Most High. It's my belief that every Christian wants to dwell there, but many don't know exactly what the secret place is or how to access it.

The Secret Place

In my own journey, I began to realize there was a reason Jesus called time with God the secret place, and I was determined to learn it. He was teaching his disciples about prayer in Matthew 6:6 and gave them these instructions: "But you, when you pray, go into your room, and when you have shut your door, pray to your Father who is in *the secret place*; and your Father who sees in secret will reward you openly."

The word *secret* there means *hidden, private*, letting us know this is something between our heart and God's. He is in the secret, hidden, private place and is waiting for us there. The world, as well as many Christians, cannot find the secret place because they're trying to relate to God with their minds, laboring intensively in the strength of their own efforts. He cannot be found that way. God and the things of the Spirit are only revealed to those who worship Him (and pray) in Spirit and in truth. (John 4:24)

The apostle Paul tells us something similar in 1 Corinthians 2:14, "But the natural man does not receive the things of the Spirit of God, for they are foolishness to him; nor can he know them, because they are spiritually discerned." In other words, we can only discern spiritual things with our spirits. Those same things seem foolish to our natural minds. But, oh, the rewards we will see (openly) in every area of our life as we spend time in the secret place!

Accessing the Secret Place

Many of us miss the awesome beauty that awaits us in prayer because we approach praying the same way we approach everything else…with the natural part of us. The natural, fleshly part of us includes our mind, body, emotions, and our five senses. Although each of these enables us to live in the natural world, they have no ability to enable us to contact God and the things of the spirit.

Our body and our five senses are not who we are. Paul calls our body an earthly tent, which is a temporary dwelling. Just as we need a space suit to exist in space, we need an earth suit to exist here on earth. When we die we leave our earth suit behind. We are eternal spirit beings who live forever. Only our spirits have the ability to contact and know God and to live and function in the world of the spirit. We do this by prayer. We live in a body created in the image of God for continual fellowship with Him. Prayer is a spiritual activity. Recognizing that we do not pray as part of a physical experience but a spiritual one is *the first secret* of prayer. It's a heart thing.

Have you ever entered into prayer and felt like you weren't accomplishing anything? Don't stop praying! To your natural mind it may seem unfruitful, but your spirit is being extremely fruitful in prayer. Never judge the effectiveness of your prayer time by what you think or feel took place. Satan will use the dry times in prayer to tempt you to quit praying, but it is in those dry times that God is working in ways you cannot see at the moment. Keep showing up every day in prayer, and you will find that on the other side of the dry period there will be the sweetest breakthrough in prayer. God wants to teach you the beauty of not being led by feelings, but knowing by faith that He is listening intently to every word you say to Him. In my dry times, He has often surprised me mid-prayer or mid-sentence with an overwhelming sense of His love and presence that is like an oasis in the desert and water to my thirsty soul.

This is part of what it means to pray by faith. Pray when you feel nothing. Pray when God doesn't seem to be speaking. Pray when it seems the heavens are brass. It may seem this way to you in your head, but know in your heart that you are indeed accomplishing much. Jesus told us that those who pray in secret or privately, God will reward openly. That isn't a maybe promise but a sure one. Notice that Jesus didn't say He would reward us if we *feel* like our prayers are answered! He rewards all who believe that what they ask in prayer is heard whether they feel like it or not. Those are the ones He will answer openly.

Let Your Heart Lead

We use our bodies and our minds to enter in to the secret place, yet they can only take us so far. For example, we have to tell our bodies to get up and go to our time and place of prayer, and they take us there. We use our physical eyes to read the Scriptures, and we use our minds to meditate on them. Our body and mind are definitely engaged, but only our spirits fellowship with God.

He created us originally for our spirits to be the king, our minds to be the servant, and our bodies to be the slave. In other words, our minds and bodies help us in prayer, but they are not supposed to take the lead. Even when our minds are meditating on the Word of God, we must ask the Holy Spirit to guide us and speak to our hearts the things He wants us to know and understand.

Our spirits are supposed to lead the way by God's own design. We are so accustomed to allowing our bodies, our feelings or our minds to take charge that it takes time and discipline to turn it around so in prayer our spirit can lead the way. The key is to ask the Holy Spirit to help us and then practice being sensitive to Him. This is how prayer changes from being need-based to being birthed from God's heart to ours.

I've found when entering my prayer time, the best way to put my mind and body in its place so that my spirit can lead is to begin with heartfelt worship and quiet meditation on the goodness and wonder of God. In those moments, my words are thoughtful and few. The more my mouth is engaged, the more my mind will take control. One of the great lessons I learned in praying is to resist the need to talk all the time.

When I first began to pray, I talked non-stop. I said everything I could think to say and then wondered why I didn't feel any closer to God. I thought this was what prayer was supposed to be. I had always heard prayer described as "talking to God," and yet, when I did all the talking my heart wasn't engaged in a real conversation. What a glorious day it was when I learned to let the Holy Spirit lead me in prayer, so I could learn when to talk, when to listen, when to worship, and when to simply sit in His Presence.

God has made a way for us to understand His mysteries by placing His Spirit in us. When we enter the secret place of His presence, the curtain is pulled back, and we can peer into the nature and ways of God. We can never in this life know Him in his fullness, but, oh, what a privilege it is to be face to face in prayer with this infinite God who created us! Just one glimpse of His goodness changes our lives forever! The glory of God awaits us, and the Holy Spirit longs to reveal Him.

In prayer, the Holy Spirit has revealed the greatest things I've ever known. In my darkest hours, I've retreated into the secret place and heard God speak a word of encouragement that gave me the strength I needed to go on. Sometimes it was just him saying, "I am with you." Yet because it was God revealing Himself to me as my constant companion and not just someone trying to pump me up, it infused me with spiritual strength.

At other times, I've been faced with a difficult decision, and it wasn't clear with my natural wisdom what I should do. While praying in the secret place, a strong sense of peace would come that I should move in a certain direction. The Holy Spirit knew things I could not know with my own wisdom, and the issue was resolved.

In John 16:13, Jesus said, "However, when He, the Spirit of Truth has come, He will guide you into all truth. He will not speak on His own authority, but whatever He hears He will speak; and He will tell you things to come." I've proven it over and over. What great joys and benefits the Holy Spirit brings to us through this wonderful activity called prayer!

Time with God

There's no better way to adjust my day than
to make my flesh stop and come in line
With prayer and praise—truly raised—
regardless of the clamor for my time.

In my own little space, seeking His face,
shut in with God, time stands still
As I worship and pray for guidance today,
I drink from a cup He has filled.

With grace and love, confidence from above,
faith and strength for the task
My day belongs to Him, not my own selfish whims;
I will do whatever He asks.

Now, I open the door, I can face life once more,
with power only His Spirit provides
When empty, I race to my special God place,
in my heart where His Spirit abides.

Donna Shelton
12/28/01

Prayer Is Our Lifeblood

As I look back over forty years of time spent in the secret place with God, I must say it becomes a more glorious journey with each passing year. It also brings a realization that there is a vast amount of knowledge about God and His ways I have yet to learn and experience. In fact, the more I know of God and His ways, the more I realize what I don't know.

I've discovered there are secrets of the secret place—this designated time and space that has been set apart for prayer. I want to share with you what God has shown me. Hopefully, each one of these wonderful truths will lead you to a deeper, more fulfilling relationship with God and will open a world of prayer that you've only dreamed of until now.

This second secret isn't hidden at all, but it's a powerful truth that's so obvious it's mostly overlooked and certainly taken for granted: *Prayer Is Our lifeblood*. Learning this secret many years ago totally revolutionized my prayer life. The enemy of our soul knows this is our lifeline and that all the power we need to live in victory is born of our relationship with God in prayer. He will do *anything* and use every weapon at his disposal to keep us from ever experiencing the joy of the secret place even one time, for once tasted, that desire will never be fulfilled by anything else!

Even as our natural body cannot survive without blood being pumped to every part of it, neither can our spiritual life exist apart from spending time in the very presence of our Creator. In His presence we find strength for living and satisfaction for our souls. In prayer, we've also been given great authority. Heaven listens when we pray. God listens! After all, we've been created in the image of God to have fellowship with Him. He wants to hear everything we have to say, and He wants to respond in such a way that we're confident we've been heard. This is why there's always a longing within each of us who truly love God to be close to Him.

The Christian who doesn't pray may do everything else, but he or she will exist with a sense of emptiness and futility. No matter what is going on around us, the grace we are given each day and the sense that all is well comes only through prayer.

Prayer is not a means to getting what we want; it *is* what we want. Time shut in with God will solve every problem, answer every question, calm every fear, dispel every worry, heal every hurt, and satisfy every longing. It will meet every need, settle every dispute, destroy every doubt, and fill every hunger. Prayer makes conquerors out of weaklings, lovers out of haters, and world changers out of nobodies. It will bring light to your day, joy to your heart, peace to your mind, and strength to your faith. This prayer, which is your lifeblood, will make the impossible possible. It will give you authority over demons, victory over sin, and boldness to be a witness. In prayer, you don't find answers. You find ***the answer!*** You find God as your priceless treasure!

Jesus explained this for us in Matthew 13:44, where He said, *"Again, the kingdom of heaven is like treasure hidden in a field, which a man found and hid; and for joy over it he goes and sells all that he has and buys that field."* Once you find God as your priceless treasure, you're gladly willing to pay the price to buy that field. God, His presence and all He has for you is the treasure. Prayer is the field that the treasure is in. You may want the treasure, but you first have to buy the field to get it.

God is that treasure *hidden* in the field for a good reason. God doesn't reveal Himself to casual bystanders or once-in-a-while prayers who consider time spent with Him as an option if they have time that day. No! This treasure of all the things I listed above is hidden in that field, so you must be willing to dig for a while until you find it. Someone might say, "I dug in that field one day and didn't find anything." Then you probably didn't dig long enough—consistent daily prayer or deep quality prayer.

The truth is, God's promised us that if we keep digging we will find Him. Proverbs 8:17 tells us, *"I love those that love me and those who seek me diligently will find me."* We all quote Jeremiah 29:11, but I love and live by verses 12 through 14. I have clung to these scriptures in my darkest trials and in times where I couldn't move forward without a definite direction from the Lord. It says, *"Then you will call upon Me and go and pray to Me, and I will listen to you. And you will seek Me and find Me, when you search for Me with all your heart. I will be found by you, says the Lord...."*

These scriptures speak eloquently and clearly about the importance of diligence in prayer. You will have to dig for a while until you find the priceless treasure of joy in prayer. The price we pay to buy that field is to show up every day with an open heart and surrendered life. Some days in prayer may feel as if you are digging yet finding nothing. God may even seem distant and your faith weak. Yet don't be deceived. God is there! Before long you will experience God like never before and receive all this glorious treasure found in Him. You will feel the difference when you are away from Him for too long, but simply lifting your heart to Him in love and gratefulness will infuse you with grace and strength.

Don't let yourself become focused on the "price of the field." If you do, you will get caught up thinking about how long it will take to see results or how much time you have to spend each day in prayer. This is what I did in those early days, and like me, you will be trying to earn something by your own efforts. If you recall, the man joyfully paid whatever the field cost *after* he found the treasure. Once your heart becomes focused on God—your treasure—by quieting yourself in His presence, joy will automatically inspire you to pay any price continually to make it yours! That will automatically open secret number three.

You, Jesus

Jesus, my relationship with You is so very precious to me.
It is something I value even more because I know what it is NOT
supposed to be.

If I were praying, reading my Bible and going to church
with the attitude that it is my "Christian duty,"
I would never have known You the way I do now.

These things are not boring or drudgery to me, but a joy.
When I wake up, I lift my heart to You and the speaking
of Your Name as I whisper,
"Good morning, Jesus" washes me with peace and joy.

I sleep and awake secure in Your love.
Your Presence never leaves me, even though I have left the intimacy
of my time with You.

If I think or breathe Your Name, You are there,
thrilling my heart once again.

It is such a joy to walk with You, to belong to You,
I don't ever want to take Your nearness for granted.

If I become so involved in the affairs of my day
that I begin to leave Your presence,
PLEASE, draw me back to the center and focal point of my existence,

YOU!

Donna Shelton
9/19/96

Secret Three

Prayer Calms the Soul

The happiest people on the planet are those who discover the joy of prayer. When we pray, our fears and worries seem to melt in the arms of Jesus, and confidence is restored. Just being in His presence renews a sense of purpose and meaning to our lives even though nothing has changed outwardly. In a world of busyness and stress, one of the greatest benefits of prayer is God flooding our soul with peace and well-being. Isn't this what we long for the most? Like the old hymn says, "When peace like a river attendeth my way, it is well, it is well with my soul."

Look at this amazing New Testament passage from The Message version of the Bible. "*Don't fret or worry. Instead of worrying, pray. Let petitions and praises shape your worries into prayers, letting God know your concerns. Before you know it, a sense of God's wholeness, everything coming together for good, will come and settle you down. It's wonderful what happens when Christ displaces worry at the center of your life*" (Philippians 4:6-7).

What if we took our busy activity, our tough decisions, our problems we encounter, and our worries and fears and shaped them into prayers as this scripture says? What if we resorted to prayer as the answer to everything?

Many times we do the opposite. We work hard trying to solve our problems, make decisions, and wrestle with our worries and fears, but we do it without the awesome power that has been made available to deal with them. *Why do we do this?* I've learned three answers to this question from my own experience. When these answers are established in our hearts, we'll stop working so hard in our own strength, and no matter how impossible the situation facing us, prayer will calm our soul when our mind wants to run wild.

1. Know Your Source

The source of all our struggles is really spiritual in nature, not physical. We are spiritual beings and the beginning of all things is spiritual. If the source of all things is spiritual then the remedy or answer to all things is spiritual. If you drive a Toyota, for example, and begin to have trouble with it, you don't take it to a Ford dealership to get it fixed. You go to the one who made it; you go to its source.

The physical world didn't create you nor the world you live in. God did! So why would you go to other sources when they don't have the ability to fix your problems? Your employer, bank, doctors, and counselors help you continue to exist in your present life, but they can't transform it. Only the manufacturer's handbook can do that. The Word of God is the manufacturer's handbook for your life!

People spend their entire lives trying to solve their problems and find purpose, fulfillment, and peace to no avail because they're going to the wrong source. God is your source! Philippians 4:19 states this clearly. *"And my God shall supply all your need according to His riches in glory by Christ Jesus."*

God will use many natural means to bless you, but always remember they are the *means* and not the *source.* God may cause you to get a promotion on the job or a raise in pay, but your paycheck is not your source. When you view your employer as your source, you will stop looking to God in prayer for your provision. This blocks the flow of heaven's blessing on your life, and you will miss out on all the surprises God has for those who trust Him. God's supply is infinitely greater than earth's supply. If God is your source and you lose your job, you will remain confident that God has many other means He can use to bless you until He provides you with another one.

Look at the Lord's Prayer in Matthew 6:10-11. In it, Jesus taught us to pray, *"Your kingdom come. Your will be done on earth as it is in heaven. Give us this day our daily bread."* He said to pray the will of heaven would be done on earth, and through this we will be provided our daily bread. Just as any good earthly father would want from his children, so God wants us to trust Him to provide for us. It brings our heavenly Father great joy when we look to Him for our provision. It's not that we're just looking to Him for material things; we, as His children, trust Him as our source for our life and everything we need. This pleases the Lord and greatly fuels our prayer time!

2. **Depend on God**

Secondly, when we depend on ourselves instead of on God, we do it without the power that's available to us. When we don't pray concerning our needs, we are saying we can handle it ourselves. In effect, we're saying we don't need God; we're smart enough, strong enough, and talented enough to come up with the solutions to our problems on our own. We can handle it. We think a little more money is all we need, or the right breaks to come our way, or getting connected to the right people. We look for a promotion or for a certain relationship to work out as the answer. This thinking is terribly misguided. None of the things you control will ever give you what you need. If we will simply pray, God will not only bring the answer to our problems—*He will show us He is the answer!*

We live in a humanistic culture that has installed humans on the throne as God. As Christians, we may reject this idea, but when we don't pray, we are humanists, too. We have placed ourselves on the throne as God, believing we can handle life's struggles on our own.

Either God is in control, or we are in control. When we don't pray, we're holding onto control ourselves and are not trusting that God knows and has what is best in store for us.

Prayer is the acknowledgment that God is our source and everything we need. Adam and Eve's tragic mistake was in believing God alone wasn't enough. The reason God told them not to eat of that one tree in the garden was that He wanted them to trust Him that what He provided was enough to meet their needs and bless them abundantly. That one tree was held in reserve so God could test Adam and Eve as to whether they would trust Him to be in control of their life and provision or if would they take control themselves. As we all know, Adam and Eve succumbed to the lie that God was holding out on them and felt the need to take their lives into their own hands. In other words, they believed the lie of the enemy that they could provide a better life for themselves than God could. We all know how that worked out!

God actually designed His plan because it's His great joy as a Father to be our source. We draw close to Him to the extent we depend on Him. When we don't spend time with God in prayer, we grow distant from Him. He becomes very small in our eyes, and we forget He owns everything. We forget He is a good Father and desires to bless us if we'll trust Him. Prayer is the act of trusting our life and future into God's hands. Prayer is believing that God knows what we don't know and can do what we can't do. So, when I pray I am acknowledging that God is on the throne, and He alone has the knowledge and power to give me the life I seek.

3. God Cares

Thirdly, when we don't have a personal revelation of how much God loves us, we'll never understand how much He cares and wants to be involved in every detail of our everyday life. That is why we struggle, coming up with ways to handle situations on our own, trying to do it in our own strength. Many Christians actually live their lives as "Christian Deists," believing in God as Creator, believing Christ died on the cross for their sins, yet carrying on their lives as if God just saved them and left them here to fend for themselves. I've even had some people tell me they didn't take a lot of things to God in prayer because they felt God wasn't interested in the small stuff, and they didn't want to bother Him. This is such a gross misunderstanding of God's nature and what the cross was all about.

Here is what is true: "*God so loved the world that He gave His only Son*" (John 3:16). God's incredible love for us was the motivating factor for Him in sending His Son Jesus to die in order to bring us back to Him. More than anything else, we must understand that God is *Father*, and as Father, He loves to care for His children and wants to be involved in the details of their lives. Jesus explained the Father's heart so clearly in Matthew 7:11. *If you then, being evil, know how to give good gifts to your children, how much more will your Father who is in heaven give good things to those who ask Him!*" He is the giver of every good gift!

Many only have a view of God as a stern ruler, someone who is angry when we fall, who wants to punish us, but that is not at all the heart of our Father. When we fall, He desires to pick us up, dust us off, and help us walk again. He deeply cares about us and wants to be involved in every aspect of our lives.

God cares when we're grieving. He cares when we've been rejected. He cares when we're afraid or worried about something. He cares when we hurt and are in pain. He cares when we're sick. He cares when we're struggling financially. He cares when we're having a difficult time in school or on the job. *He cares!* Not only does He care, but also He alone has the power to help us in our time of need. When we bring our needs to God in prayer, it is the ultimate statement that we believe He cares.

First Peter 5:7 reiterates this by saying, "*casting all your care upon Him, for He cares for you*". Jesus states it beautifully in Matthew 6:30-33, which says, "*Now if God so clothes the grass of the field, which today is, and tomorrow is thrown into the oven, will He not much more clothe you, O you of little faith? Therefore do not worry, saying, 'What shall we drink?' or 'What shall we wear?' For after all these things the Gentiles seek. For your Heavenly Father knows that you need all these things. But seek first the kingdom of God and His righteousness, and all these things shall be added to you."*

Childlike Faith

I went before the throne of Grace
and looked into my Savior's face.

There, in prayer, I spoke with Him and shared my heart
as friend with friend.

He listened to me with love-filled eyes,
then Wisdom spoke and filled the skies
With words of life in answered prayer,
I opened my heart to receive them there.

His smile turned to laughter as He saw my struggle
to receive the answer without any trouble.

He said, "Don't let go of your childlike faith,
expecting as they do with upturned face.

A child knows for sure that I will answer each prayer
for he has no doubt that I really care.

So, let this same confidence be resident in you
and I'll delight in showing just what I can do.

Donna Shelton
12/22/85

Secret Four

You Have the Desire to Pray

I believe every Christian wants to pray, yet for many the struggle of maintaining a consistent prayer life is very real. To overcome this, and the guilt and condemnation that comes along with it, there are truths we must recognize. When we do even the acknowledgment of them brings freedom.

When we give our life to Christ, His Spirit comes to abide in our hearts and produces a longing to be with Him. We were created for fellowship with God, and prayer *is* fellowship with God. This is the most open secret of all. It's where we belong. We were not created for work, play, doing chores, eating, and entertainment. All of these things are parts of our lives, but they are not the reason we were made. We were made for communion with God. That's the reason we are most at home when we pray. Prayer makes everything right.

If spending time with God in prayer is so wonderful, why do we struggle to maintain a consistent prayer life? Many Christians live under condemnation because they have been told they *ought* to pray. We will never discover the beautiful life of prayer by doing it out of duty or obligation. In fact, being told constantly that we should pray without discovering how to pray actually drives us away from prayer.

Prayer is not a law; it's a *relationship*. For example, I enjoy spending time with my wife, not because I'm told to do so but because I want to do so. I love her. If I came home to my wife with a list of things I was supposed to do—tell her I love her, hold her tightly, kiss her, and so on—she would think I'm crazy. Yet, ironically, we do this with God when we come to Him with a prayer list. This is legalistic praying. Is it any wonder then, why prayer like this is so unfulfilling?

If I were to ask you if you love God, I'm sure you would say "yes." If I were to ask you if you want more of God in your life, I'm confident you would say "yes." If I asked you if you want to be closer to God than you are presently, I'm sure you would say "absolutely." Well then, you can pray!

We don't need a list of rules when praying. Talking with God is about a love relationship. Prayer is simply being with someone we want to be with. When we complicate prayer with rules and obligation, it loses its beauty. The conversation becomes one-sided, consisting mostly of asking for the most pressing needs to be supplied.

Many times when people begin praying, they feel it hasn't done any good because they ran out of things to say. Yet, remember this! When you spend time with someone you love, you don't always have to have something to say. Think of times when you've been with a friend and didn't talk much at all. Sometimes it's enough just to be with them in unspoken companionship. True friends can be together without having constant conversation.

When you're with a friend, do you do all the talking? I hope not! I hope your friend also talks while you listen. Being quiet and listening is part of the relationship. Both of you want to be heard and both of you want to share things that are important to you. It's the same way when we commune with God through prayer. Just showing up and being with Him is sometimes enough. We talk, and we listen. Sometimes it's enough to just sit quietly in His presence. Other times our heart is full of things to pour out to Him, and because we know He's listening, we anticipate what He will speak to our hearts.

We put too much pressure on ourselves to perform while we are in God's presence. Some time we just need to be quiet and listen. For instance, some days while in prayer, I have been tired and didn't feel like saying much. I just opened my Bible and let God minister to me through His Word the entire time. Usually this will end up with me being inspired by something I've read and cause me to respond with a time of worship.

One time I was leading an early morning prayer meeting at our church, and I was so very tired having been up late the previous night. During the prayer meeting, I fell asleep in front of all the people. When I woke up, I looked around, and everyone was gone. The prayer meeting had long been over. When I looked down, I saw that someone had placed a blanket over me with a handwritten sign that read, "Good Morning, Pastor." I was so embarrassed, and said, "God, I'm so sorry. Did this time in prayer count?" I'll never forget what God so gently said to me: "Well, at least you showed up!"

I'm not advocating sleeping in prayer, but this made me realize that as long as we show up with our heart open and desiring to be there, we are in God's presence. Remember, God looks at the heart, not our great ability to pray. We need to throw out the rules of obligation and just spend time with our wonderful Savior Jesus.

Spiritual Hunger

We must understand spiritual hunger because our spirit gets hungry just like our physical body does. Actually, there are some interesting parallels between hunger and prayer. For instance, the more we pray, the more we want to pray. The less we pray, the less we want to pray. It's like eating dessert. The more often we eat it, the more we want to eat. The less we eat dessert, the less we want to eat it.

Notice how David describes His hunger and thirst to be with God in Psalm 42.

"As the deer pants for the water brooks, So pants my soul for You, O God. My soul thirsts for God, for the living God. When shall I come and appear before God?"

There is a longing, a hunger, and a thirst inside each of us that can never be satisfied apart from time spent with God. We can busy our lives and time with many things, trying to fill that hunger, but it will never fill the place that belongs to God alone. When we give place to that spiritual hunger deep inside us and turn to God in prayer, we will be satisfied!

This is why Jesus told his disciples in John 6:35, *"I am the bread of life. He who comes to Me shall never hunger, and he who believes in Me shall never thirst."* Jesus is the bread of life! In those days, bread was so nutritious that a person could survive as long as they had bread and water. Everyone knew that and it's why the statement was meaningful. He's the real deal! So much of what we fill our lives with is not real "bread." It's junk food!

When we are bored, we find something to do. We turn on the TV. We find something that needs to be done around the house. We head to the refrigerator to find something to eat. We're "hungry," but nothing seems to satisfy us because it's our spirit that's hungry, and we're mistaking it for another kind of hunger. It's a wonderful day when we learn to distinguish when our spirit is hungry and reach for Living Bread instead of other things!

Years ago, I went on my first prolonged fast. It was twenty-one days with only water. For the first week or so, my body was crying out for physical food so much that I didn't have a great time in prayer. I thought, *This isn't working. I feel more distant from God than when I was eating.* But after a number of days, my body finally quieted down. The physical hunger was gone. Once my physical hunger quieted down, my spirit came alive in a whole new way. I felt so hungry for God. My times in prayer were wonderful. I would sit in the presence of God and not want to leave. I felt so close to Him!

Spiritual hunger was there all along, but the voice of my physical hunger had drowned out the voice of my spiritual hunger. The satisfaction I was getting from the presence of the Lord was so much sweeter and fulfilling that I thought, *If I could keep fasting for the rest of my life, I would!* It made me realize exactly what Jesus meant when His disciples questioned Him as to why He wasn't eating. He told them He had food to eat that they didn't know about (John 4:31-32). He wasn't fasting on purpose at that time, but doing the will of the Father filled Him to the point that natural food lost its attraction. Through this God-called fast, I was given a glimpse of this, and it has stayed with me to this day.

I had another interesting revelation as my fast came to an end. For my first meal, my wife made me a bowl of tomato soup. When I took the first little sip, it tasted like the sweetest ice cream sundae I had ever eaten. Before the fast, this soup would have tasted very bland to me and it would have never been my first choice of something to eat. I hate to admit it, but I loved French fries and soda and they were my first choice of food. Several days after ending the fast, I sat down at a restaurant to eat my first meal of solid food. Of course, I ordered French fries and a soda and couldn't wait for the familiar wonderful taste of them. It was a total shock when I took the first bite of a French fry. I almost spat it out! It tasted like cardboard. It was even more of a shock when I took the first drink of the soda. It tasted like pure chemicals. I hated it!

What happened? The things that I hungered for and thought were so tasty before tasted horrible to me. I learned an important lesson through this. When we fill ourselves with junk food every day, we develop a taste and hunger for it even though it's not real or nutritious. If we ever cleanse our taste buds through a period of fasting, we will develop a hunger and taste for that which is real and nutritious for our bodies, exposing the junk food as fake.

In the same manner, our spirit is hungry for that which is real food, time with God, worship and seeking to obey Him. When day after day, we continually fill ourselves with only the junk food of busyness and entertainment, we will develop a greater hunger and taste for those things over time spent with God. Eventually, we will come to the point where it seems like those are the right things to fill our time.

They taste like real food to us. The problem is the more we fill ourselves with the junk food of this world, the more it robs us of our hunger for the real food found in the presence of God.

This is why it's so hard to pray. It is why the time we do spend with God in prayer and His Word seems so dry and unprofitable. We have lost our taste for spiritual things. Then, we go through the motions out of duty, but there is no joy in it. We begin praying with good intentions, but are soon bombarded in our brains with thoughts of so many other things we could be doing. Our spiritual taste buds need to be cleansed. We don't realize it, but the junk food is destroying our spiritual vitality.

Let me tell you what it's like when you're eating the bread of heaven, Jesus Christ. You get up in the morning and start your day with God. You go somewhere quiet with your Bible in hand. You say good morning to Jesus, tell Him how much you love Him, and begin to worship Him just for who He is. Then, you thank Him for all He's done and is doing in your life, and invite the Holy Spirit to enlighten His Word to you today. You read a passage of Scripture and meditate on it. You prayerfully ponder it until something in it speaks to you. At that point you may stop and spend the rest of your time there, or the Spirit may lead you to go on. He may illuminate many things to you in this one passage. You ask God what He wants you to do with what He has spoken to you. If it's something to be believed, then believe it with all your heart. If it's something to be done, then do it with all your might!

I hope you can see now that prayer is not a monologue; it's a dialogue. It's sweet communion between you and the Father, Son, and Holy Spirit. It is great to ask God to give you a burden, or deep compassion to pray for certain people and situations in your city and the world. It brings great satisfaction to your own soul to be an instrument that God can use to pray for others. This little exercise is also a sure way to keep you from becoming focused on 'all about me'. It is also empowering to know that when you are in sweet fellowship with God, you have great power in prayer to ask God for things to change in people's lives and in the world.

When your time in prayer is coming to an end, don't rush out of His presence. Some of the most wonderful times are experienced when you are just sitting there and soaking in His presence and worshipping Him.

There is nothing laborious or boring about true heartfelt prayer. When you rise up out of prayer, set your mind to obey God throughout the day. Don't just pray in the morning and then forget about God the rest of the day. Acknowledge Him throughout your day, and do whatever He says. This is what Jesus calls "abiding in Him." This is praying without ceasing. This is what it means to turn talking with God into walking with God!

Union with Christ

"Now, more than ever before, you must begin every day with an earnest reaching out to Me. I hold your every moment in My hand. If your life is to count for anything, then you must depend on Me to guide every moment and approve every action. It can be done.

I have placed this burning desire deep inside you to live your life in such union with Me that you can sense My heart and yield, almost unconsciously, to My leading in every life situation that faces you. You are My hands extended in help and comfort and My voice, speaking words of encouragement and wisdom for those who are confused about My ways - this is my heart for you.

Many belong to Me, but have never discovered the wonder of walking with Me day by day, confident of My continual presence and guidance. There is a sweet unspoken fellowship, an unconscious awareness that I am ever near, and peace, that I long to cover their hearts with. "

"Lord, this, then, is my prayer. May I repeat it in my heart over and over during the day."

'Stand in the center of my heart, Lord. Rise up in me if my thoughts stray very far from You at any time of the day. Help me to continually practice Your Presence, that I may commune with You constantly - in and about everything I do or say or see.

Lead me, convict me instantly of wrong thoughts and motives, and help me to repent quickly without excusing my behavior.

Make me strong, very strong, with quiet determination that moves in obedient self control, yet, will face every enemy without flinching—especially, Lord, the enemies of my own soul—sin, selfishness, pride! You alone can deliver me cleanse me and keep me clean. My heart cries out to You, My wonderful Savior! You are my Hope, my Rock, I cling to You.

I give this moment to You, Lord. The next hour is not mine to give. But as I walk into it, help my heart to unconsciously yield it to You, and the hour after, and the hour after that.

I need You desperately!

By Your grace, I will do what has been put into my hands for this moment - as unto You - be it great or small, because, Jesus...I really, really love You!

Donna Shelton
1996

Is God Listening?

Shutting the Door

Remember in Matthew 6:6 quoted earlier, Jesus said when we pray, we have to shut the door. The secret to shutting the door is two-fold. When we enter the place of prayer, we must shut out everything except God. We must forget all the things we have to do and leave behind all the other things our mind has been preoccupied with. When we enter into prayer, our biggest enemy will not be the devil, but rather a wandering mind.

Have you ever noticed when you begin to pray that the smallest things distract you? For instance, you may see a fly on the wall and start thinking, How did that get in here? *Are there more? Where is my fly swatter? I can't stand flies!* In that moment, you have left the secret place you were just entered. As soon as you realize your mind has wandered, take charge of it and consciously bring your focus back to where it was before the distraction grabbed your attention. I always apologize and ask the Holy Spirit to help my thoughts and words stay focused.

It's often wiser to take your actual Bible into your time of prayer rather than your cell phone, but with so many versions of the Bible and a multitude of reference books at your fingertips, many use their phones or iPads instead. It takes a lot of practice and commitment to keep that time sacred and not answer a text, a call, or look at a notification of news that pops up. At least mute the ringer on your phone while in prayer; that helps tremendously when you're talking with God.

Before you pray, try to make every possible provision to ensure you will not be interrupted even though you may think this is impossible. Think about a businessman going into a meeting with someone very important. He will tell everyone ahead of time that he cannot be interrupted no matter what. We must remember *who* we're meeting with when we enter into prayer. We're meeting with God—the Creator of the universe—the One who made all those "important people." He deserves not to be interrupted.

Sometimes we treat God as if He was less important than someone on the phone! Reverence is something the Church knows little about today, yet the Bible is clear that we're to approach God with reverence and godly fear (Hebrews 12:28-29). I think one of the reasons people find prayer difficult and dry is because they treat it too casually. In other words, they don't "shut the door." When we shut the door in a meeting, we're indicating that the meeting is important and we don't want any interruptions. It's the same way in prayer. We should "shut the door" to interruptions and distractions to show reverence to God. If prayer is something we just try to do if we get time, and then when we pray we're distracted because our minds wander and our hearts are half into it, we're showing disrespect for our meeting with God.

Reverence is still important today. The laws of the Old Covenant have been fulfilled in Christ, but notice they have been fulfilled, not done away with. As born-again believers, the law is now written on our hearts instead of stone tablets. In the Ten Commandments, the law that says, *"You shall have no other gods before Me"* and *"I am a jealous God"* is still valid.

Today that law is written in the heart of every believer. When we come before God, we must shut out all things that compete for our allegiance. This is a Holy God we're meeting with, and He deserves to be approached with reverence and godly fear. We must "shut the door!"

We are to enter the secret place with deep reverence and honor. When we worship, we should pour our hearts out honestly before Him. When we open our Bibles, we must read the Scriptures with deep respect for His Word. Then, we will sit in awe of Him, listening for what He has to say to us, instead of talking all the time. When we make requests, we'll be careful to do so according to His will. We'll ask what's on His heart today. We'll ask about what and for whom He wants us to pray. Then, before we leave, we worship Him, thank Him, and wait silently (the hardest part). We simply sit and enjoy being in His presence. It's from this place that grace and peace are found to cover our day no matter what comes.

Jesus demonstrated the art of prayer in more places than the Lord's Prayer. Mark 1:35 tells us that Jesus rose long before daylight, went to a solitary place and prayed there. Luke 5:16 also tells us that He *often* withdrew into the wilderness to pray. Jesus knew how to shut the door. Both the places He prayed, a solitary place and the wilderness, speak of closing the door. In other words, He *withdrew.* This word speaks volumes to me about His prayer life. He removed Himself as far as possible from anything that would distract Him, and shut Himself in with the Father.

It's interesting to note that Jesus rarely prayed long prayers publicly. When faced with a need, He would say, "Go!" "Be opened!" or "Be still!" Jesus' public authority came from His private time with His Father where He had withdrawn to a private place and "shut the door." He prayed long prayers privately and was empowered in private to be used by God publicly.

I have a feeling that when people pray long public prayers they're trying to gain the ground that should have been won in their private time with God. Much time spent with God in the secret place secures a confidence in who you are in Christ and gives you great boldness against the enemy. All of life's issues are settled and all victory is won in the secret place with the door shut.

Reverence and the Fear of the Lord

Earlier we touched on the disappearing concept of reverence. Reverence is awe that exposes our shame. When we see God as He really is, it causes us to see who we are without Him. *Reverence* means, *to bow the face down in submission and respect.* Reverence acknowledges that God is holy, and we are not. In other words, we are not coming to Him as our equal.

There has been a lot of emphasis on the idea that God is our friend. With that as our way of thinking, we hang out with Him and the rest of our friends at church. Then, when we disobey Him or fall into sin, we assume He understands and just kind of winks at it. Yet God is not just a buddy we hang out with. Yes, Jesus is our friend, but He is also our Lord. He paid a tremendous price for our sins and our disobedience. He paid with His very life and blood! That alone should be a cause for reverence.

Never mistake the fear of the Lord as being the same as natural fear. Fear in the natural is tormenting and oppressive, but fear of the Lord is a high respect for God. Reverence and godly fear don't make us afraid of God but are born out of love for Him. True reverence and fear of the Lord inspires heartfelt worship and humility in His presence. It helps us give Him the undivided attention He deserves.

When I think of coming before God with godly fear and reverence, I'm always reminded of Moses' first encounter with God at the burning bush. He learned at that moment that even the place he was standing on was holy because God's presence was there. As he stood before the burning bush, the Lord said, *"Do not draw near this place. Take your sandals off your feet, for the place where you stand is holy ground."* (Exodus 3:5). Taking the sandals off of our feet speaks of the deep humility that is required to approach God. Moses' sandals had collected dirt from his daily walk, so he had to humble himself and take them off as he approached God.

We must understand what a holy thing it is to close the door in prayer, where you and God are alone, face to face. We cannot treat it as a casual, common thing. There needs to be a deep respect and appreciation for this awesome privilege we have as imperfect, mortal humans to commune with our Creator, the Ruler of the Universe. Just think of this! We, who have no righteousness of our own, get to fellowship face to face with the infinite, all-wise God who upholds all things by His Word. We don't deserve to be there on our own, but thank God, through the sacrifice of Jesus on the cross, He has given us the same right standing He has with God! When we fully grasp this, it will astound us and produce humble reverence within our heart. How deserving He is of our reverence and godly fear!

Now add this scene out of Isaiah 6 to the reverence you already have, and it will be sealed in your heart the same as it was in Isaiah's.

> In the year that King Uzziah died, I saw the Lord sitting on a throne, high and lifted up, and the train of His robe filled the temple. Above it stood seraphim; each one had six wings: with two he covered his face, with two he covered his feet, and with two he flew. And one cried to another and said: 'Holy, holy, holy is the Lord of hosts; The whole earth is full of His glory!' And the posts of the door were shaken by the voice of him who cried out, and the house was filled with smoke.

What a scene! Isaiah sees the Lord on a throne—high and lifted up. This was no casual friend Isaiah was hanging out with. This was a God who was worthy of all his worship and even his life!

Your prayers will only rise to the level of your view of God. If your view of God is small, your prayers will be small. If your thoughts of God are small, your problems will be big. If your faith is small, it's because your God is small to you. Therefore, the first order of business in developing a healthy prayer life is letting the greatness and majesty of God awe us into a state of reverence. We are not invited into God's throne room because we are worthy. We are invited into His throne room because He is so merciful to us that He has provided a way through the blood of Jesus for us to enter there. Because of this, we never forget what a profound privilege it is to be in the secret place

Father, Son, and Holy Spirit

In the scripture from Isaiah above, the angels cried, *"Holy, holy, holy is the Lord of hosts. The whole earth is full of His glory."* Have you ever wondered why the angels cried *holy* three times? Wasn't one *holy* sufficient? There are many valid theories, but I believe that this instruction was also an acknowledgment of the holiness of the Trinity. One was for the Father, one for the Son, and one for the Holy Spirit. It's important we are aware of the worthiness of all three to be worshipped.

The Father dreamed His great plan for our lives. He's the one who loves us so much He gave His only Son to die for us. Basking in His love for us is one of the most important parts of our prayer life. Humbly worshipping Him for an unconditional love we don't deserve enriches our soul and leaves us forever grateful. If we spend time studying and thinking about His love, worship, and adoration will automatically burst out of our souls!

Jesus willingly gave it all up to become flesh like us. He walked in our shoes, felt our pain, and ultimately suffered the most brutal death imaginable to purchase us back for the Father. These thoughts are so deep that all the books in the world could not sound the depths of this amazing act of love. Do you understand how utterly lost we would be without Him, how helpless and hopeless we would be for eternity? The more we cultivate and delve into these thoughts, the higher and more passionate our worship will be.

Before Jesus ascended to heaven, He told the disciples it would be *better* for them when He left because He would ask the Father to send the Holy Spirit to live in us. Jesus called Him the *Helper* and told His disciples that the Spirit of Truth would dwell within them.

And I will pray the Father, and He will give you another Helper, that He may abide with you for ever- the Spirit of truth, whom the world cannot receive, because it sees Him not, nor knows Him: but you know Him; for He dwells with you, and will be in you.

John 14:16-17

We don't often think of the Holy Spirit in the same way we think about the Father and the Son. He is the third person of the Godhead, with all the same attributes and nature of deity as the Father and the Son. The Holy Spirit is the One who carries out in us all the Father has planned for us and all the Son has purchased for us. Without the presence of the Holy Spirit in our lives, we would be left to figure out on our own how to carry on this Christian life. We need Him desperately!

There's no true advancement of the kingdom of God without the Holy Spirit. Jesus said the Holy Spirit is another One just like Himself. Everything Jesus did in His earthly ministry, the Holy Spirit can do through us. Can you see how important it is to be aware of the precious Holy Spirit in us and be sensitive to His voice?

We ignore Him to our own detriment. Some wrongly view the Holy Spirit as a cloud or an anointing on our lives, but He is a *person* with all the qualities and attributes of personhood. He speaks, feels emotion, thinks, and acts. In fact, He can be grieved! We are commanded in Ephesians 4:30 not to grieve Him, *"And do not grieve the Holy Spirit of God, by whom you were sealed for the day of redemption."* Just think about ignoring someone who lives in your own house. How offended and grieved would they be? Yet, we are the *temple* of the Holy Spirit, and He lives in our *house.*

When we're not sensitive to the presence of the Holy Spirit and carry on our lives as if He was not there, He is grieved. In 1 Thessalonians 5:19, we are told not to "quench the Holy Spirit." To *quench* means, *to put out the fire.* The Holy Spirit keeps the fire of our love burning for the Lord. Disregard for the Holy Spirit has produced many cold, dry Christians.

Years ago, as our church became very large and gained influence around the world, I decided we would become a more conservative church. I played down the gifts of the Spirit and no longer talked about the Baptism in the Holy Spirit. Speaking in tongues out loud during the church service was no longer acceptable. After a year or so this way, I began to notice that I didn't sense the presence of God in my prayer time or my preaching as I had before.

One day I asked God, "Where are You? Where have You gone?" and I'll never forget His reply. He said, "You cannot have Me if you don't want what I do. If you're ashamed of what I do, you're ashamed of Me!"

I was deeply convicted because I realized that unknowingly, I had grieved and quenched the Holy Spirit. I quickly repented and I thought, *Surely God will restore His presence to our services and in my prayer time the same as before.* I was wrong. I prayed and wept for five long years asking God to restore His Spirit in my life and church as it was before. God was merciful and true to His Word. People were still being saved and helped through the Word being preached. I felt the difference, though, and it was unacceptable to me. I became desperately hungry and thirsty for that treasure that had to be found again. Even if it took the rest of my life, I determined I would never stop hungering and thirsting until I was filled once again. It isn't the same for everyone, but this is the way it was for me.

Suddenly, one day the heavens opened and the Holy Spirit gloriously baptized me in His presence once again! It felt the same as when I was first born again, and I was like a little child in His presence. I wept and laughed and was overcome with the joy of sensing His tangible presence so wonderfully after five long years. I returned to the pulpit the following Sunday and there was a wonderful anointing on my preaching. The Holy Spirit fell on the entire congregation. During the sermon, people fell to their knees crying out to God. Weeping could be heard all over the church. The Holy Spirit had returned!

I don't know why God withheld His Spirit in that way for those five years, but I can tell you it made me oh so hungry and even desperate for the presence of God. I promised Him I would contend for the power and presence of the Holy Spirit both in my private life and public ministry for the rest of my life! I now have a deep, abiding respect and appreciation for the Holy Spirit and will never, ever take His sweet presence for granted.

If your love for God has grown cold and your spirit has become dry, could it be that you have grieved and quenched the Holy Spirit? You need Him to fill your prayer time. You need Him in order to make right decisions. You need Him in order to resist temptation and live a life pleasing to God. You need Him in order to minister to the needy around you. You need Him in order to fulfill what God has called you to do. My dear friends, I beg of you to realize what has been lost and return to your first love. The Holy Spirit is worthy of our worship and His presence is to be desired above all else.

When you have a revelation of what it means to shut the door and bask in the beauty of the love and care of the Father, Son, and Holy Spirit, the next secret I learned will open to you as wonderfully as it did to me.

Staying Connected

Good Morning Father.
I want to walk with You all day,
staying connected in every possible way.

I have opportunities, a dozen or more
to continue this conversation by shutting the door,

Closing out the noise of the situation I am in,
to speak to You directly – time and again.

In these small moments as life rushes on...
my heart remains connected to You all day long.

Donna Shelton
1/16/02

Secret Six

Entering God's Presence

One day, while meditating on the passage from Matthew 6:6 where Jesus tells us to go into the secret place, the words *your Father who is in the secret place* jumped out at me. At that point, I realized our Father is already in the secret place. He doesn't show up after we get there. He is already there!

Many times we pray trying to get God's attention. It's as if we're trying to earn the right to be heard because of the way we feel as we begin our time of prayer. We don't recognize unworthiness is trying to make us feel the need to impress God somehow so He will show up in the secret place. That mentality will have you feeling like you're alone or just talking to the air as if God wasn't there. I used to think I had to pray for twenty minutes or longer to earn my audience with God. I would say, "Oh, God, please come and meet with me. I need you." I would keep praying like this and would be exhausted before He ever "showed up."

Now I realize how ridiculous this was. He doesn't need to come anywhere. He was there in the secret place before I was. This may seem like a small thing, but it completely changed the way I prayed. Now, I shut the door, sit down, and begin by acknowledging His Presence. I might say, "Father, it's so good to be with You." Knowing that He's already there waiting on me, and looking forward to this time as much as I am, changes my praying. I know He already accepts me and is listening even before I say anything. Many times I will just sit and envision Jesus sitting across from me. Oh, what sweet communion, what praise and adoration flood out of my soul! It is God and me, alone in the secret place, and I love every moment of it.

What a revelation it was when I realized I didn't have to beg Him to meet with me but that I have been invited into His presence. Jesus said in Revelation 3:20, *"Behold I stand at the door and knock. If anyone hears My voice and opens the door, I will come in to him and dine with him, and he with Me."*

This scripture is written to Christians—not the lost. We're not knocking at His door trying to get Him to open it and meet with us. He's knocking at the door of our hearts. This picture has always astounded me! Just imagine the Creator of all things is standing at our door, waiting for us to get up and open it. Then the moment we open the door, He is there.

He wants to dine with us and us with Him. Think of that. When we pray, it's time to feast on His presence and He on ours. It offends our precious Lord when we beg for Him to come meet with us when He already said He would never leave us. Actually, it accuses God of lying to us. Oh, how much our Lord and Savior longs to meet with us in prayer!

The apostle Paul had a great revelation about this and explained it this way in Romans 10:6-8, *"But the righteousness of faith speaks in this way, 'Do not say in your heart, "Who will ascend into heaven?"' (that is, to bring Christ down from above) or, "Who will descend into the abyss?"' (that is, to bring Christ up from the dead). But what does it say? 'The word is near you, in your mouth and in your heart' (that is, the word of faith which we preach)."*

Paul felt so strongly about this that He said we don't ever need to say, "Lord, come." He is already with us, in our heart, and in our mouth. The first words on our lips in prayer should be with great confidence that God is present. He's waiting! He's listening! Anything less is a display of false humility. To enter the secret place requires us to approach Him in faith, believing that He is there. He wants us to remind Him of His promises to us.

The Bible gives us all the encouragement we will ever need to have confidence in prayer and assurance that He's listening. Hebrews 4:16 instructs us to have this attitude in prayer. *"Let us therefore come boldly to the throne of grace, that we may obtain mercy and find grace to help in time of need."*

Come boldly! It's a throne of grace. We are worthy to enter the throne room. This sounds blasphemous to the religious mind, but we are worthy because the very righteousness of Christ has been bestowed on us because of His blood that was shed on our behalf.

Sometimes we focus too much on who we are not, instead of who Christ is and what He has done in us and for us. Reverence is not groveling in the throne room. It's not a denial of the price Christ paid for us on the cross. Don't tell God you don't deserve to be there. He knows that already and that's why He sent His son to die for you. He looks at you through the sacrifice of His Son. Because of that, you do deserve to be in His presence. Wallowing in unworthiness in prayer is saying to God there's something more *you must do* to earn the right to be there. You are in effect saying the cross wasn't enough. Do you see what an offense this is to the grace of God?

Be reverent, but pray bold prayers. Pray big prayers! Pray with confidence. God is already there waiting for you!

Your Presence

Some may stumble, some may fall,
some may give up and not try at all
to abide and stay in Your Presence.

But, oh, what a treasure awaits all who seek
who diligently come to sit at Your feet
if they abide and stay in Your Presence.

Donna Shelton
1/19/97

---Secret Seven---

You're Beautiful to God

My wife is absolutely beautiful! But, when she gets dressed in the morning, I can tell whether she feels attractive or not by the way she carries herself. When she doesn't feel attractive, I have to convince her of how beautiful she is regardless of how she feels. Her beauty has nothing to do with what she's wearing or what kind of hair day she's having. Her real beauty is inherent; it's who she is.

We encounter this same problem in prayer. How we view ourselves and how we view God determines what our time in prayer will be like. We carry ourselves differently into the secret place when we feel "attractive" to God. If we have a "bad hair day" spiritually, we feel unattractive to Him. We crawl into our prayer time feeling unworthy. We tell ourselves that God is reluctant to meet with us. We spend a great portion of our time with Him trying to make ourselves attractive. We point out our faults and failures. We tell God how unworthy we are. We have repented of all known sin, but we struggle to forgive ourselves.

Have you ever spilled something on your clothes, and all day, all you can think of is your soiled garment? Even though it's a small spot that nobody notices but you, you feel unattractive and self-conscious all day. It's the same way when we enter the Throne Room focused on a spot on our robe of righteousness that has already been washed by the blood of Jesus. This is a great hindrance to prayer.

The truth is, God sees us as beautiful even when we do not feel attractive. We make a major mistake when we think God sees us the way we see ourselves. Oh, how differently we approach our Father in the secret place when we feel "attractive" to Him. Psalm 103:11-14 NLT should give us all the confidence we need to approach Him daily with the confidence of a child with his or her loving father.

"For his unfailing love toward those who fear him is as great as the height of the heavens above the earth. He has removed our sins as far from us as the east is from the west. The Lord is like a father to His children, tender and compassionate to those who fear him. For He knows how weak we are; He remembers we are only dust."

Just think about that phrase, "He has removed our sins as far as the east is from the west." God is infinite, which means He cannot be measured. We could spend the rest of our lives heading east or west looking for our sin, but we will never find it. It is nowhere to be found. It has been removed. If we have truly repented of our sin, no matter how great or bad it was, it's gone!

We must learn to forgive ourselves of what God has forgiven us. Many people still think there's a spot or stain of sin that the blood of Jesus could not remove. They feel like they have to live with that spot forever. This is accusing Jesus' blood of not being strong enough to remove every stain.

Through the prophet, Isaiah, God says, *"Come now, let's settle this,"* says the Lord. *"Though your sins are like scarlet, I will make them as white as snow. Though they are red like crimson, I will make them white as wool"* (Isaiah 1:18).

He is saying, "Dear child, you are not thinking correctly about your sin and the blood of Jesus. No matter how stained your garment has become, nothing can resist the cleansing blood of Jesus. It makes the worst sinner as pure and white as snow.

Our own robe of self-righteousness is as filthy rags. But through the cleansing blood of Jesus, God has given us a new robe to wear, the righteousness of Jesus Christ. We should never live our life trying to pay for what's already been paid for on the cross. *"For God made Christ, who never sinned, to be the offering for our sin, so that we could be made right with God through Christ"* (2 Corinthians 5:21 NLT). Because of this, we can always come boldly and with confidence into the throne room, knowing we belong there!

We come boldly to the throne, not because of who we are, but because of who Jesus is! When the devil accuses us of being unworthy as we enter the secret place, all we have to do is remind him of our standing invitation, stamped with the blood of Jesus. He is our advocate, our attorney, and He is at the right hand of the Father standing up for us. His blood has been poured over the mercy seat of heaven.

When the devil tries to accuse, saying, "Look what they have done," Jesus points to His own blood on the mercy seat and says, "No, look what I have done! My Father sees them as I do, clean through My blood."

Be done with fear and intimidation. Be done with insecurity and unworthiness. Be confident and bold, and let faith arise in your heart. Talk to the Father as a beloved child, not as a beggar. Pray big, mighty and powerful prayers! It gives the Father great pleasure when His children are confident of who they are in His son, Christ Jesus. If you have any doubt about it, spend time reading and meditating on Romans 8:31-39 where Paul explains in great detail that *nothing* can separate you from the love of Christ.

God is Unlike Any Earthly Father

Our boldness in the throne room comes from confidence in the Father's love for us. In my early years in prayer, I viewed Him as a hard taskmaster who was mad or disappointed with me because of my faults and failures. I was trying to live a Christian life, but felt I would never be good enough to measure up to His expectations. This wrong thinking hindered me from receiving His grace, which I needed be who He wanted me to be. That empowering grace could only be received by approaching the throne of grace boldly.

Many times this wrong view of God comes from equating Him with our earthly fathers. Many children have grown up with earthly fathers who withheld their love and acceptance unless it was earned. Others never felt loved at all because their fathers were either non-existent or mistreated them terribly. It then becomes difficult to picture our heavenly Father as totally different from our earthly one.

Our Father in heaven is not like any earthly father. They may give gifts with strings attached. They may be self-centered. They may give love, but it's for their own benefit. Many times men don't know how to be good fathers because they didn't have a good father. Our heavenly Father is not like that at all.

Look carefully at this verse in Matthew 7:11 where Jesus explains just what our heavenly Father is like. He is contrasting Him, not with bad fathers, but with good, earthly ones. He says, *"If you then, being evil know how to give good gifts to your children, how much more will your Father who is in heaven give good things to those who ask Him?"*

"If we want to have a good relationship with our heavenly Father, we must first forgive our earthly fathers. We must do what Jesus did on the cross. He said, *"Father, forgive them for they don't know what they are doing."* We must realize our earthly fathers didn't know what they were doing to us. Some of you may say that isn't true and you can't forgive. You may want them to pay for what they did to you. I can tell you for sure this attitude of unforgiveness will only hold you in bondage and prevent you from being able to receive God's love for yourself.

One time in an evening service at our church, a man had a powerful encounter with God. He fell to the floor under the power of God. As he was on the floor with his eyes closed, he started making motions with his hands as if he was a child playing with cars. This seemed very strange to all who were watching. But when the man got up from the floor, he tearfully explained that when he was a child, his earthly father never let him play with toys. In fact, he was never allowed to play at all or even own a toy! His father was very serious all the time and made him work from the time he was very young.

When he was on the floor, the Father told him, "I am not like your earthly father. I love you unconditionally, and I want to heal you of your past wounds." He then gave him a toy car and said, "Here, I want you to enjoy yourself." The man said that all the wounds of the past melted away as he played with the toy his heavenly Father gave him. His life was completely changed that night!

This may seem like a strange story, but it demonstrates how loving, kind, and generous our Father in heaven is toward us. He is not a hard taskmaster who wants us to perform for Him all the time. He wants us to bask in His amazing love for us!

God is a perfect father! He is the kind of father we were supposed to have all along. Hebrews 12: 5-11 explains this. When He disciplines us, it's not for His benefit, but for ours. Think about that. We can trust Him. Everything He does is for us. He doesn't discipline us because He's mad at us. He disciplines us because He loves us and wants the best for us. God doesn't withhold His love from us when we mess up. We don't have to earn His love. It is unconditional. He loves us just as much on our worst days as He does on our best days. With that forever settled, just think how much this correct view of God changes our time in the secret place. No longer do we have to spend unfruitful time doing penance, trying to earn His approval. What we have is so much better – His faithful, never-ending love!

The Real Heart of the Father

The most beautiful story of the Father's love for us is found in a familiar parable Jesus told his disciples. It perfectly illustrates the heart of the Father. Jesus tells of a man who had two sons. The younger one asked his father to divide up the inheritance he would receive when the father died. He wanted his portion then. The younger son then left for a faraway country where he quickly wasted all his inheritance on wild living. No sooner did he do this than a famine struck the land, reducing him to hunger and forced labor, feeding pigs.

There with the pigs, Jesus tells us this young man came to himself. He realized that while he was starving, even his father's lowest servants had plenty of food, so he decided to go home. He was probably rehearsing his apology speech when his father spotted him still a long way off.

Let's carefully observe this illustration of how our Father sees each and every one of us:

> "When he was still a great way off, his father saw him and had compassion, and ran and fell on his neck and kissed him. And the son said to him, 'Father, I have sinned against heaven and in your sight, and am no longer worthy to be called your son.' But the father said to his servants, 'Bring out the best robe and put it on him, and put a ring on his hand and sandals on his feet. And bring the fatted calf here and kill it, and let us eat and be merry; for this my son was dead and is alive again; he was lost and is found.' And they began to be merry."
>
> Luke 15:20-24

This most beautiful story of our Father's love for us is often read casually, like a familiar tale. Yet this story like no other contains a picture of the depth of the Father's love that is almost incomprehensible. The prodigal son *willfully* left his father's house and squandered all of his inheritance on wasteful living. He shunned his father's love. If there was anyone who ever disappointed his father, it was this young man. Even when he decided to return home, he still didn't have the right motives. He returned home simply because he was hungry!

He felt that his sin had disqualified him from His father's love and his place as a son. In the same way, when we fall into sin and squander our Father's inheritance we grow distant from God. We become lazy in our prayer life or stop having those wonderful times with Him in prayer altogether. When trouble comes, we come to our senses and pray, usually out of desperation. We want our relationship to be like it was, but feel we have disqualified ourselves from our place as a son or daughter at His table. This causes us to come before Him with a servant mentality, where we must earn our way back into the place we left, instead of coming to Him as the beloved, redeemed child of God we are.

When the prodigal's father saw him coming, he had compassion, ran, fell on his son's neck, and kissed him. The father didn't wait for the son to grovel, begging for acceptance. Before he could get the words of repentance out of his mouth, his father was already showering him with love. What a picture this is of our heavenly Father! Can we see this is our Father's posture toward us?

Notice carefully what happens next. The father did let him get the words out of his mouth, *"I have sinned and I am not worthy to be called your son."* The acknowledgment of both of these truths was very important. *"I have sinned"* was confessing his sin and his desire to turn from it. *"I am not worthy"* was an acknowledgment that he didn't belong in his father's house. Because of the guilt and shame, he felt disqualified from being called *son.* All he could hope for was to be a servant. That is where the father stopped him and this is where our heavenly Father stops us.

When we fall into sin and repent, God also forgives us and restores us into right relationship with Him because Jesus is worthy and has paid for our sin. Even as this father did, so does our wonderful, loving, forgiving heavenly Father do when we return to Him. He says, *"Quickly, put the robe of righteousness on my child. Get the ring of sonship that signifies he is a full heir of his Father's inheritance and put it on his finger. Put new sandals on him. My child is going to have a new walk. I have places for him to go and things for him to do. I'm not finished with him yet. I'm going to use him to do great things for Me."*

Then God says, just like the father said to his prodigal son, "Let's throw a party! My son was dead, but he's alive again. He was lost, but now he's found. Let's celebrate!" I hope you get this. If your heart is right and you have truly turned from your sin, then the secret place immediately becomes a place of celebration. You don't have to spend the next few weeks working yourself back into a place where you feel comfortable in the presence of God. See yourself in prayer, wearing that robe of righteousness, the ring of sonship (whether you're a son or a daughter), and new sandals on your feet. The moment you enter the prayer room, see your Father running to you, hugging, and kissing you! Oh, what love this is!

God is 'in Love' with Us!

God loved us before there was anything lovable about us. He doesn't love us because we are good sons and daughters. He loves us *simply because* we are His sons and daughters.

"But God showed his great love for us by sending Christ to die for us while we were still sinners" (Romans 5:8).

We've heard "God loves you" and have said it so much in casual conversation it has all but lost its meaning. There's nothing more important than having a deep, clear understanding of God's love for us. Everything in our lives is built on this one thing! I've often told people if you're struggling with insecurity, fear, or unworthiness, you don't really know by experience God's love for you. You need to forget everything else. Stop studying about prayer, faith, end times, or anything else and immerse yourself in a deep, thorough understanding of everything the Word of God says about His love. Nothing is as important as this. Everything else will be wrong if it doesn't emanate from God's love for you.

Love doesn't begin with us; it begins with God! He loved us first (1 John 4:10-11). When we try to love God before experiencing His love for us, we'll fail miserably. The only ability we have to love Him comes from experiencing His love for us. Love for God that isn't rooted in His love for us leads to dead works. We will work hard to love Him, but it will never feel like it's enough. Our love will always fall short. It is God's love for us, not our love for Him that holds and keeps us.

Also, it's impossible to truly love others unless we're totally secure in His love. We only have the ability to love others if we've experienced for ourselves. Philippians 2:1-2 NLT says, *"Is there any encouragement from belonging to Christ? Any comfort from His love? Any fellowship together in the Spirit? Are your hearts tender and compassionate? Then make me truly happy by agreeing wholeheartedly with each other, loving one another with one mind and purpose."*

Have you ever felt your Father's arms of love wrap around you and comfort you in a moment of loss, betrayal, or trouble? I'm talking about *the real experience* of His love, not just the theological idea of His love. If you have, then you can love others out of that same experience. Once you've experientially felt God's affection for you, then you'll be able to feel that affection and mercy for others as you comfort them. Many have a theological belief in God's love for them, but are not experiencing it daily on a personal level.

> May Christ through your faith [actually] dwell (settle down, abide, make His permanent home) in your hearts! May you be rooted deep in love and founded securely on love, That you may have the power and be strong to apprehend and grasp with all the saints [God's devoted people, the experience of that love] what is the breadth and length and height and depth [of it] [That you may really come] to know [practically, through experience for yourselves] the love of Christ, which far surpasses mere knowledge [without experience]; that you may be filled [through all your being] unto all the fullness of God [may have the richest measure of the divine Presence, and become a body wholly filled and flooded with God Himself]!
>
> Ephesians 3:17-19, AMP

Notice the language Paul uses in trying to describe this love that is "rooted deep in love and founded securely on love." A passing thought about this love will not do. We need supernatural power to grasp this love. Many think they grasp it, but they don't.

Paul said to grasp the *experience* of that love, not *knowledge about* that love. Love exists in four dimensions. People think we live in a three-dimensional world, but since we're spirit beings, *this love* can only be grasped in the fourth dimension of the world of the spirit. Our head will never get us there. A whole world opens up to us when we walk in the experience of God's love for us. There's a place awaiting every believer that's so wonderful, so filled with the divine presence of God, that our being becomes wholly filled and flooded with God Himself.

Have you ever spent time in prayer until this actually happened? This is what awaits you when you grasp the breadth, length, height, and depth of His divine love for you.

Do You Love Me?

In a very touching and intimate story after Jesus' resurrection, Peter struggles with understanding God's love. Jesus asked him:

> Simon, son of Jonah, do you love Me more than these?" Peter answered, "Yes, Lord; You know that I love You." Jesus replied, "Feed my lambs," and then He asked the question of Peter again: Do you love me? Peter replies again, "Yes, Lord; You know that I love You." So Jesus said to him, "Tend My sheep." Then, a third time Jesus asks if he loves Him. It says, "Peter was grieved because He said to him the third time, 'Do you love Me?' And he said to Him, 'Lord, You know all things; You know that I love You.' Jesus said to him, 'Feed My sheep.'
>
> John 21:15-17

When Jesus asks Peter, "Do you love Me?" He uses a brand new word for love: *agape*. *Agape* is God's supernatural love. Jesus was asking Peter, "Do you understand how your love for Me comes out of My supernatural, unconditional, unending love for you? This love has nothing to do with your ability to love Me, but everything to do with My ability to love you."

Jesus was restoring Peter from his terrible failure when he denied Him three times. So, three times Jesus extends agape or God's supernatural love to him, by saying, "Peter, your failure doesn't affect My love for you. My love for you has nothing to do with you."

When Peter answers, "I love you," he uses the word *phileo,* a common word in that day. *Phileo* means *affection, brotherly love, or friendship.* In other words, Peter was saying, "Lord, I have affection for you as a friend, but I know nothing of this agape you are talking about. Lord, I want to know Your love, but I still can't grasp it. I'm doing my best to love You."

Notice, the emphasis was on Peter rather than Jesus. *Agape* originated out of God. *Phileo* originated out of Peter. The third time, when Jesus changed his question using *phileo,* Peter was grieved because he knew Jesus was acknowledging that he didn't get it yet. He just couldn't grasp that this agape love, was not affected by his failure, his denial of Jesus. He couldn't grasp that this agape had nothing to do with himself but everything to do with Jesus.

What kind of love doesn't change at all when we fail miserably and are at our worst? Only Agape! God's love never changes. The human love we're used to isn't like that at all. We withhold love when people hurt or disappoint us, and we make them earn our love again. How can we possibly understand a love that's totally unaffected by what we do, good or bad?

A few weeks later, Peter stood before the masses at Jerusalem and boldly proclaimed the Word of God. There was no sense of condemnation or unworthiness in him then. He had gotten it! He knew through experience the revelation that God didn't just love him as a friend, but was "in love" with him, forever, no matter what.

Another picture of our love relationship with God is found in Song of Solomon 4:1: *"Behold, you are fair, my love! Behold, you are fair!"* There are two words that stand out to me in this verse. He says *my love.* God calls us *His love.* When you think about it, saying, *I love you* is vastly different than saying, *You are My love.* This means I don't just love you, but I'm in love with you.

Some men resist this talk of intimacy when it comes to a relationship with our heavenly Father, but they need to get over it. They will never have the proper relationship with God without seeing Him "in love" with them and them "in love" with Him.

John Bunyon, the author of the classic, *Pilgrim's Progress,* had been struggling with condemnation and a sense of unworthiness. Then he heard someone preach from this verse in Song of Solomon. On his way home one day, the words *You are My love, you are My love,* began to kindle in his spirit repeating over and over. He was trapped between hope and fear saying, "But is it true; is it true?" On one side, hope had him thinking, *This might be true. If it is, it's amazing! I am His love!* But on the other side, fear had him thinking, *But it can't be true. Look at me. I'm a failure. I'm so unlovable. The only experience of love I've had from my parents and friends has disappointed me.* His heart wanted to believe it, but his head was rejecting it. *If we're really His love, it changes everything!*

Then God took Bunyon to Romans 8:31-39:

"What then shall we say to these things? If God is for us, who can be against us? He who did not spare His own Son, but delivered Him up for us all, how shall He not with Him also freely give us all things? Who shall bring a charge against God's elect? It is God who justifies. Who is he who condemns? It is Christ who died, and furthermore is also risen, who is even at the right hand of God, who also makes intercession for us. Who shall separate us from the love of Christ? Shall tribulation, or distress, or persecution, or famine, or nakedness, or peril, or sword? As it is written: "For Your sake we are killed all day long; We are accounted as sheep for the slaughter." Yet in all these things we are more than conquerors through Him who loved us. For I am persuaded that neither death nor life, nor angels nor principalities nor powers, nor things present nor things to come, nor height nor depth, nor any other created thing, shall be able to separate us from the love of God which is in Christ Jesus our Lord."

As these words sank in, he exploded inside with comfort and joy. Suddenly he was able to believe that he was totally forgiven and that God was *in love* with him!

This is one of the things we struggle with the most. We grasp the fact that God loves us, but it's much harder to grasp—much less say with confidence—that He's "in love" with us. This is why we struggle to accept the fact that we're *totally forgiven* of all sins and failures before and after we were saved.

In Ephesians 5:25, Paul gives us an interesting insight to this love God has for us. He insinuates the only way to understand it is to compare it with marital love—husbands are to love their wives as Christ loves the Church. I think we all would agree it would be wrong for me to tell anyone besides my wife that I'm in love with her. We tell many people we love them, but saying "I'm in love with you" is reserved for marriage. This is a completely different kind of love.

In biblical marriage, the husband is no longer to live as if he were a separate person from his wife. His life is inextricably bound to her, and she to him. The two are one. All his decisions are to be made with her best interest in mind. He is to be completely devoted to her, even to the point of laying down his life for her. He comes to know her with an intimacy reserved only for her. Even though he loves other people such as their children and friends, he's in love with only her. She is so secure in his love that she's unashamed to be her true self around him. She lets him know things about herself that she would never trust anyone else to know.

Husbands and wives are free to be completely naked and vulnerable before each other. As long as Adam and Eve walked in communion with God, they were naked and not ashamed. But once sin brought a separation between them and God, their first response was to hide their nakedness because they were afraid. They were ashamed. When you enjoy the experience of being in love with God, you can be completely naked, totally vulnerable before Him and not be ashamed. You can trust Him to know things about you that you would tell no one else. He already knows everything about you anyway, but your openness and honesty before Him in prayer is very precious to Him.

You know all His decisions are with your best interest in mind. When you have a bad day or do something stupid, you know He's not going to divorce you. His love doesn't end. The only difference in this relationship and the one of marriage is, when death comes, we aren't parted with Him as we are with our mate. Instead, we see Him face-to-face. This is called a mystical union. The mind cannot grasp it. When someone falls in love, everything about them changes. They become like a child when talking about their love. When you ask them to explain it, they can't. They just say, "I'm in love."

If your Christian life has been boring and dry, if prayer has been a drudgery and dutiful obligation, I urge you to find the God who doesn't just love you, but who is in love with you. Once you do this, everything will change. There will be a glow about you. You will become like a child when you talk about Him and to Him. When people ask you to explain it, you'll say, "I don't know, I'm just so in love with Jesus." How sweet the fellowship, and what comfort and consolation you will experience in the secret place when you walk in the revelation that God is in love with you. You will no longer go there to ask a few things of a distant God. You will enter His presence to spend time with the One you are in love with and who is in love with you!

There's an amazing story in the Old Testament where God tells the prophet Hosea to marry Gomer, a prostitute, in order to send a message to His people. After he marries her, Gomer continues to sleep with many other men. Of course, Hosea is broken-hearted over this, but he goes from house to house wherever she had been, leaving provisions for her. He was constantly wooing her back to himself, even though she continued to reject his love. Finally, when she returned home, he received her with open arms as his wife. Their entire story was a parallel of God's relationship with His people who strayed from Him again and again.

God was not ignoring their sin. He told them the longer they continued in their sin, the more of His judgment they would incur. Even so, He wanted them to know that all their sin had not caused Him to stop loving them. It's the goodness of God that leads us to repentance. Don't think you're getting away with your sin just because God is providing for you and everything seems to be going along just fine. He's being kind and patient with you because He is in love with you. *But don't mistake His love for weakness!* This is God, the Infinite Ruler of all things you are dealing with. Don't spurn His love any longer. It will cost you dearly. Return home today to the arms of your Love!

Don't take His love for granted. This great love is very costly. It cost your heavenly Father the life of His only Son in exchange for yours. Grace is not cheap, but it's free because of the price Jesus paid. We are attractive to God, not because of who we are, but because of who Christ is in us. Prayer is a precious privilege afforded us by the mercy of God.

Enter the secret place with deep gratitude. Let this love humble you in His presence. The fact that we've been invited to fellowship with the creator of the universe is worthy of us taking every possible opportunity to kneel with a thankful heart, just for the privilege of being there.

You Are in Love with Us

Every desperate heart, every longing soul
Every troubled mind, longing to be whole

You can hear their every cry, even when they do not call
And yet, You long to help them, fill their void, become their all

The love You have for all You've made I'll never understand
Rejection doesn't faze You, because You have a plan

You never get discouraged or think the price You paid too great
And if they still ignore Your call, in patient love You wait

...Until they come...

Donna Shelton
©1999

Secret Eight

Waiting on God

One of the things we find most difficult today is just being quiet. We're so addicted to noise and activity that we're uncomfortable with silence. Everywhere we go there is noise. At a restaurant or the mall, it's not enough to have the sound of all the people. Music is playing in the background. We have the radio on while in the car. We turn the TV on when we get home. We so seldom experience silence that many of us don't know how to handle it and sometimes even feel depressed if we experience total quietness for any length of time.

Another word we're not very familiar or comfortable with today is *solitude*—simply being alone. Many are even afraid to be alone. When we're by ourselves, we jump on social media to talk to all of our Facebook or Instagram "friends." I don't have time here to talk about how unhealthy this is for our lives in general, but more seriously, it robs us of the most important place of silence and solitude in the presence of God in prayer.

Jesus addressed this in John 15:4-5, 7 when He told the disciples how vital it was that they stay connected *to Him.* How much more does it apply to us when we're bombarded constantly with distractions. Jesus said, *"Abide in Me, and I in you. As the branch cannot bear fruit of itself, unless it abides in the vine, neither can you, unless you abide in Me. I am the vine, you are the branches. He who abides in Me, and I in him, bears much fruit; for without Me you can do nothing. If you abide in Me, and My words abide in you, you will ask what you desire, and it shall be done for you."*

Apart from Him, we can do nothing. This is astounding! He said that everything we do depends on this—abiding in Him. What does that phrase even mean? *Abiding in Him* means to settle down, remain, and make our permanent home in God. We don't just enter prayer to read a scripture and ask God for a few things. We are to take up residence there!

Think of being at home. Sometimes we're talking, sometimes listening, and at other times we just sit silently doing nothing. We are home; we can let our guard down and be ourselves. There is no pressure to perform. We are just there. What if we could be this way in prayer? What if we could let our guard down and just be ourselves with no need to perform? We would sometimes be talking, sometimes listening, and other times simply sitting silently in the presence of the Lord, doing nothing.

It's this "doing nothing" while in our time of prayer that we have a problem with most. We always feel the need to be doing or saying something. We're conditioned to think we're not being productive when everything is quiet and nothing tangible is happening. We don't think this is prayer at all, yet this time of quiet, peaceful silence can be a most productive time with God. This is waiting on the Lord. Many times, this is when we hear Him speak profoundly into our hearts. His voice can finally be distinguished from all the noises we hear.

Jesus said if we abide, remain, and make our home in the Him—the Vine—we'll be fruitful in our lives. I know these words *abide* and *remain* don't sound very exciting. We live in a culture of instant gratification that thinks we should get what we want and get it right now! We have lost the art of waiting. If we don't learn to wait, settle down, and remain in the presence of God, prayer will not yield the results we expect. Prayer does change things, but that's not the ultimate reason we're there. Prayer is first designed to change us!

The Deceit of Distraction

In Luke 10:38-42, we read of Martha inviting Jesus to her home. She was distracted, making a big dinner for Him while her sister, Mary, sat at His feet listening. Martha complained to Jesus about Mary not helping, but calling her "dear Martha" Jesus explained that her sister had chosen the better activity. Hearing what He had to say was the one thing that was most important.

What would your answer be if you were asked, "What is the one thing that would make your life better and meet your needs right now? Many would answer that they need to make more money. Others would say they need a better house or car. Some would say they just need the right relationship. These things may be important to us, but focusing on them are really distractions. They are not really what we need. There is only *one thing* we really need—to learn to sit at the feet of Jesus and let Him speak to us through His Word. Jesus addressed this in Matthew 6:31, by telling us not to worry about what we eat or wear and not to let these things dominate our thoughts because our heavenly Father is fully aware of all of our needs. He said if we would seek Him and His Kingdom above all else that "all these things" will be provided for us.

One of the enemy's most effective strategies is to get us distracted with busyness and wanting this or that. Our fast-paced lives have become so filled with activity we hardly have time to think, let alone pray. We tell ourselves we can't stop because there's so much to do. We go, go, go from morning to night and then wonder where the day has gone. Maybe we had even planned to pray, but the time just got away from us.

My dear friends, we are deceived. It's not that we don't have time to pray. It's not even that time gets away from us. We don't understand what the *one thing* is that we need most! When we have one thing we know has to be done before the day is over, we always find a way to do it. We will arrange or rearrange everything else to make sure it's done. Our problem is that most of the time we don't remember what our very most important "one thing" is.

Jesus let us know through this story that the most important thing for us is to sit at His feet and hear His Word. If we really believed this, we would push everything else aside to make sure it happens. If we don't stop lying to ourselves, saying we're too busy to stop everything else in order to sit at Jesus' feet, we'll continue to live frustrated, unfulfilled lives. There will never be enough time in our day to stop everything else and spend time with Him. This may sound hard, but I'm trying to help you have the life you really want.

There is a reason spending time with Jesus is the one thing needed. *Everything else we need flows out of it.* Prayer sets everything right, calms our souls, and gives us the grace to tackle all that life throws at us. Trying to live without prayer is like trying to drive a car without putting gas in the tank. We would never say, "I know the tank is empty, but I don't have the time to stop and fill it up today. I have too much to do." We would soon find ourselves stranded by the side of the road, frustrated and not accomplishing anything we had set out to do. So many things seemed more important until we didn't have the fuel to get us there to do them. In the end, the crisis we faced was of our own making by not putting first things first.

Spending time with God in prayer is the one thing that gives us the fuel, the grace, and the instruction we need to accomplish everything else we need to do. Just as a car needs gas, God has designed us to need Him. He created us in His image to have fellowship with Him. God breathed His very breath into the nostrils of Adam, and as God's Spirit went into man, he was given life. That Spirit in us yearns and longs for the presence of God. Living in communion with Him is what breathes breath into our daily lives and provides the grace to meet every need.

The psalmist describes this so beautifully. As you read the Psalm below, take note that David is not making a theological statement, but he's telling of an experience in his daily life.

One thing I have desired of the Lord, That will I seek: That I may dwell in the house of the Lord All the days of my life, to behold the beauty of the Lord, and to inquire in His temple. For in the time of trouble He shall hide me in His pavilion; in the secret place of His tabernacle He shall hide me; He shall set me high upon a rock. And now my head shall be lifted up above my enemies all around me; therefore I will offer sacrifices of joy in His tabernacle; I will sing, yes, I will sing praises to the Lord.

Psalm 27:4-6

Notice all the blessings and benefits that flow out of his time with God. But none of these were the one thing he desired and sought after. The one thing was just to be with God in the house of prayer and behold the beauty of the Lord. This thrills my soul! Only those who have found the secret place know the overflowing joy he is talking about. Sure, he also inquired things of the Lord, but that's not what brought a song to his heart.

Once you've beheld the beauty of the Lord in the secret place of His tabernacle, nothing else matters. God does fight your enemies, and He removes some of your problems, but the ones He doesn't remove seem to be of no account anymore for you have found your place in Him. This is the place where you were born to be. Oh, I wish I could take you by the hand and lead you to this place, but every person has to find it for himself or herself. Do you want to go there?

Praying Through the Dry Times

The Bible is full of scriptures admonishing us to wait. When we ask God for something, there's always a span of time between asking and receiving. God is a gardener God—not a genie God! Yet we want to use prayer as a lamp we rub, make three wishes, and get everything we want. If this how we view prayer, we will be sorely disappointed. God is a gardener, and our individual lives are the field He is cultivating. Growing a garden takes time. Lots of time!

Jesus gives us a great picture of a life of prayer in Mark 4:

And He said, "The kingdom of God is as if a man should scatter seed on the ground, and should sleep by night and rise by day, and the seed should sprout and grow, he himself does not know how. For the earth yields crops by itself: first the blade, then the head, after that the full grain in the head. But when the grain ripens, immediately he puts in the sickle, because the harvest has come."

Mark 4:26-29

We go to sleep at night, rise every morning, and spend time with God in prayer. Some days it seems all of heaven is open to us, and on others it seems like nothing is happening. We go through seasons where it seems our prayers aren't getting answered and the breakthroughs aren't happening. We wonder if it's doing any good. Rest assured that God is working; we just don't know how. He's working "underneath the ground," deep in our hearts, even though we can't see the evidence of it yet.

God is working on us as we wait upon Him so we can bear fruit. The end game of prayer is not so much to get God to do something, as it is to get us to the place where *we* can do something. God is not so much interested in blessing us as He is making us into someone who can be a blessing to the world. Of course, we will be blessed, because we must be blessed to be a blessing.

Blessings and breakthroughs always seem to come suddenly. The victory will surely come, but it's timing is not in our hands; it's in God's. Jesus is the Lord of the harvest; we are lords of the seed. When and how the harvest of our praying comes is in God's hands. It's our business to keep planting and watering the seeds of prayer, trusting the results into God's hands. This is the attitude of a heart waiting on God in prayer.

We must have a clear understanding that this is God we're dealing with, not another man. Prayer is not a negotiation between God and us; it's a complete surrender to our Maker. He is Lord! He determines the rules of this relationship. It was a great day when I discovered that He is God, and I'm not. He is bigger than my brain. He knows things I don't. He is all wise, all-powerful, and everywhere present. It is an easy thing to lay down my life before Him when I have a full grasp of who it is I'm dealing with. I give Him full control. I embrace the truth that His plan is what's best for my life, and He's the gardener cultivating the best in me.

Saying an 'Eternal Yes'

I never took my relationship with God very seriously as I was growing up. I met my wife, Donna, in college and fell in love with her. When I asked her to marry me, she said she loved me but she couldn't marry me. She said, "You tell everyone the one thing you will never do is become a preacher. When I was fourteen years old, I completely surrendered my life to God, and He told me I would marry a preacher. So, I can't marry you."

Another thing that bothered Donna was that the Dean of Students at the college we attended told her to stay away from me. The Dean told her that she could tell I had not said an "eternal yes" to God. At this point in my life, I didn't even know what an "eternal yes" was. I claimed to be a Christian, but I didn't want God running my life. I wanted to be in control of my future.

Eventually, through prayer, Donna felt God was giving her permission to marry me. For the first three years of our marriage, I was still insistent that I would run my own life, not God. We sang in church, and I taught a class here and there and felt pretty good about my service for Him. But as time went on, I became frustrated and miserable. I didn't know this was God dealing with me. Finally, I came home from work one day, fell across my bed, and started crying uncontrollably. I said, "God, what is wrong with me? I can't take it anymore. What do You want with me?"

Immediately, I had a vision. I saw a blank piece of paper with a place for a signature at the bottom. I asked, "God, what is this?"

"This is My will for the rest of your life. Now, sign it," He answered.

"But if this is a contract with You that I'm signing, it needs to be filled in so I can know the terms of this contract," I said.

"No! Sign it, and then I'll fill it in," He said. I suddenly understood the true meaning of Lordship.

God doesn't tell us all the plans He has for our lives today, so we can decide whether we want to do them or not. In the vision, I saw myself pick up a pen and sign this blank piece of paper. I knew this was a life-changing moment. I was saying "Yes!" to whatever God would later write on the page, trusting that He knew what was best for my life.

As soon as I put the pen down, I heard God say, "Now, go preach the gospel!"

"God, I *knew* You were going to say that!" I responded.

But the paper had been signed, and the decision had already been made. It didn't matter what God wrote on the page, I had already said an eternal yes. The reason I didn't want to be a preacher was that I thought my life would be miserable. I had bought into the lie that I knew what was best for my life. I had no idea of the joy and fulfillment that awaited me being in the center of God's will.

Here I am more than forty years later, and I can tell you that saying an eternal yes to God is the only way to live. Don't hold anything in reserve. Complete abandonment to His will is the only way to wait upon God. As we wait in His presence and meditate on His Word, God will plow the soil of our lives. This may be hard on the flesh, but the dealings of God are always sweet to the spirit. He may be dealing with a bad attitude one day, selfishness another.

Many times, prayer seems fruitless because we miss what God is doing. Prayer is not to be led by us, but by God. When you read the Scriptures, let God highlight what He wants you to focus on that day. Don't rush into prayer with all you want to accomplish. Wait upon Him until you hear His heart. God always has something on His mind. It's our job to find out what that is!

God may want to plant seeds of faith in your heart. You may be asking Him for things you want to happen, but your trust must remain in Him whether it happens or not. In prayer God always must be in control—not you. Waiting is being sensitive to what the Gardener wants to do in you today. We are product driven, but God is process driven. We want every moment to produce something for us. God wants to work a process in us. Prayer is a process. As you wait upon Him, be patient as He works His process in you.

Pruning

At some point, God may be interested in pruning you. The pruning process is interesting. We don't prune or cut back a plant because it's not producing anything; we prune it because it *is* producing something. We prune the plant or tree so it can bear even more fruit. This is the part of God's process many people don't understand. For instance, we may have finally experienced some success and gotten things the way we want them, and then God starts cutting us back. We feel we should go from one success to another, but God knows how prone we are to become complacent or prideful, trusting in our success. He is constantly working on us to keep our trust in Him, not in ourselves. This may seem undesirable to those who have not learned the secret place, but I have come to love God's correction as much as His blessings.

God chastens us because He loves us and He does it for our profit (Hebrews 12:5-10). If it's God who is chastening, we will feel loved and embraced by Him. The loving hand that holds the pruning scissors is cutting on our souls for our benefit, to grow us. Learn to love the conviction and discipline of God. Waiting on God is laying our whole life fully in His hands. He has a life prepared for us that's far better than the one we have prepared for ourselves. Trust the Gardener!

How to Wait

So, how do we wait upon the Lord? Actually, I must be careful here because if I were to give you a set of rules, you would never find this secret place of waiting. In one sense, I cannot teach you how to wait on the Lord. I can only tell you what I've experienced and then give you a few tips to show you the way into this secret place.

Some of my greatest experiences of waiting on God have been through meditation of scripture. For example, I will be reading a passage of scripture, asking the Holy Spirit to speak to me, when a certain sentence or thought will jump out at me. I take this as God speaking to me. I will meditate on the passage over and over. I will begin to talk to God about it, asking Him what it means for my life. Then I often find God speaking to me about some area of my life. As I respond with a heart of surrender to Him, His presence becomes evident in the room.

Anytime God's presence shows up, I respond with more worship. In these moments, time seems to stand still as I just wait in His presence. It seems like nothing is happening. In fact, it's at these times *the most* is happening.

I sit still, pondering the goodness and majesty of God. As long as His presence is there, I will wait. Many times, people pray until the presence of God shows up, and then once it does, they get up and leave. When we do this, we miss some of the most beautiful and rewarding times in prayer!

One of the easiest ways to get into a time of waiting on God is through worship. I like to pick a passage of scripture that focuses on some aspect of the person of God. This could be focusing on Him as Creator or focusing on His nature, such as His infinite wisdom or power. I have meditated a lot on His infinite love and mercy. Sometimes I'll sit and ponder on the wonder of Jesus and His sacrifice on the cross. (The important thing is to pick out something very specific. Don't just think about God in general.) These specific aspects of our wonderful God—Father, Son, and Holy Spirit—will expand our meditation like nothing else and inspire heartfelt worship. As I worship Him, thinking on a specific aspect of who He is, His presence fills the room. Then I find myself sitting, overwhelmed by His presence, with my thoughts on Him the entire time.

All this activity—meditating on scripture, worshipping, and sitting quietly in His presence—are a part of waiting on God, but don't let this become a formula for you. Regardless of what you experience during prayer, it's always good to sit quietly and reflect on the things that have happened during these moments. As your time comes to an end, it's also good to see if there's anything else God wants to speak to you. Whatever you do, *never just rush out of your time with God.* Always, end your prayer respectfully.

Here is a passage where David describes His own process of waiting on God:

O God, You are my God; Early will I seek You; My soul thirsts for You; My flesh longs for You In a dry and thirsty land Where there is no water. So I have looked for You in the sanctuary, To see Your power and Your glory. Because Your lovingkindness is better than life, My lips shall praise You. Thus I will bless You while I live; I will lift up my hands in Your name. My soul shall be satisfied as with marrow and fatness, And my mouth shall praise You with joyful lips. When I remember You on my bed, I meditate on You in the night watches. Because You have been my help, Therefore in the shadow of Your wings I will rejoice. My soul follows close behind You; Your right hand upholds me.

Psalm 63:1-8

All these things are expressions of a heart waiting on God in prayer. You can see that David's prayers were not based on a legalistic formula. I love to meditate on the phrase, "I have looked for you in the sanctuary" found in verse 2. This is a great picture of prayer. It's a picture of our hearts looking for God in prayer, in the scripture, in worship, and in our intercession for the world. Oh, how glorious it is when we find Him!

Of course, God has been there all along. It's not that He hasn't been there and all the sudden walks into the room. But, many times in the secret place, there does come a moment when God's presence becomes manifest or tangible. Even though God has been there all the while, we experience His presence in a very real, close, and obvious way. Many Christians never know what it's like to experience the manifest, tangible presence of God.

God desires to reveal Himself to His children, but we must seek Him out and expect Him to show up. Jesus promised us if we love Him and obey Him, He will manifest Himself to us (John 14:21). This has to be the greatest promise in the Bible! When we walk in the manifest presence of God, the grace and favor that comes with the presence gives us everything else we need.

The Bible is very clear that spending time with God is waiting on Him in prayer. In the past, when we were an agricultural society, the family worked hard during the day and then came home. They waited for mom to cook a good home-cooked meal and then sat down together to eat. They would spend the evening out on the porch, enjoying being together as a family, or they might find a quiet place to read one of their few books. Prayer was much easier in those times because they were accustomed to quietness and solitude. They weren't rushing the kids to soccer practice or watching their favorite television series.

> Be still, and know that I am God; I will be exalted among the nations, I will be exalted in the earth! The Lord of hosts is with us; The God of Jacob is our refuge.
>
> Psalm 46:10-11

Be still!

It's very clear that we'll never really know God until we still our souls in His presence. Don't complicate this theologically by trying to figure out what He meant when He said "be still." *Be still* simply means what it says. Find a quiet place alone and shut all thoughts of anything but God out of your mind. It may be very hard to quiet your mind at first, but if you discipline yourself to stay there with your Bible open in your lap, eventually your mind will quiet down. Being still doesn't mean to empty your mind; it simply means you fill it with thoughts of God. We need to learn to be still!

Be Still and Know

Sometimes we don't allow God to enlighten our minds with His Spirit because we don't know how to be still long enough for Him to speak to us. We are spiritual beings who live in physical bodies. Either the spirit is active and in charge or the body is. When the body, which includes the thoughts of our minds and our emotions, is the most active, it drowns out the voice of our spirit.

There are two kinds of knowledge: *acquired knowledge* and *revelation knowledge*. *Acquired knowledge* is what we know and learn through our five senses. Our minds are constantly being bombarded with thoughts, especially through our eyes and ears. Of course, we need this knowledge to live our daily lives, but this knowledge will not help us when it comes to knowing God and His plan for our lives. For these things, we need revelation knowledge.

Revelation knowledge is knowledge God reveals to us by the Holy Spirit. Although revelation knowledge comes through reading and meditating God's Word, it's not the accumulation of thoughts about God that we're talking about. Revelation knowledge comes when the Holy Spirit illuminates a passage of scripture to us as we meditate on the Word. One moment it doesn't mean anything special, and the next moment it does. It is like a light bulb being turned on, causing us to see something we didn't previously understand.

The primary definition of *revelation* in scripture is *to uncover or reveal something that is hidden.* It's like pulling back a curtain so we can see what's behind it; we couldn't see it before because it was hidden. As that happens, we have not just come to understand a bit of information, but we have come into contact with God through His Word. We have come to *know God* in a way we didn't moments before instead of just knowing something *about* Him.

Paul said everything he knew about God had come, not through knowledge he had acquired through study, but God had revealed Himself to him (Ephesians 3:1-5). Paul calls this a mystery. Remember, a mystery is not something that cannot be known; it is something hidden that must be revealed. In other words, these things are hidden from our natural minds. Our intellects will never find God. How can we possibly grasp the things of God unless the Holy Spirit reveals or uncovers them to our spirits?

The humanist or materialist will never find God because he believes that the physical realm is all that exists. He only believes what he can process with his rational mind. Sadly, many Christians fall into this same trap. They say they believe in God but live their lives as if all the issues they face have natural origins needing natural remedies. It's no wonder these people say God never shows up in their lives, and they never hear God speaking to them.

God has chosen to hide Himself from the natural mind for a very good reason. If man could find Him through his own wisdom and efforts, he wouldn't need God. I believe we should study to be as intellectually astute as possible about the things of God, but ultimately, all our wisdom and knowledge must be laid at the feet of Jesus, acknowledging that He far surpasses human knowledge. The only way we can truly know Him is if He reveals Himself to us. This is something the apostle Paul understood and prayed for us.

> Therefore I also, after I heard of your faith in the Lord Jesus and your love for all the saints, do not cease to give thanks for you, making mention of you in my prayers: that the God of our Lord Jesus Christ, the Father of glory, may give to you the spirit of wisdom and revelation in the knowledge of Him, the eyes of your understanding being enlightened; that you may know what is the hope of His calling, what are the riches of the glory of His inheritance in the saints, and what is the exceeding greatness of His power toward us who believe, according to the working of His mighty power.
>
> Ephesians 1:15-19

God wants us to understand our calling in life, Christ's inheritance for us, and the infinite power of God that is ours through Christ. We'll never live this scripture because of how many times we've read it, and we don't need to be a Bible scholar to have a spirit of wisdom and revelation. We just need to be still in God's presence, meditate on the

Word, and ask the Holy Spirit to reveal it to us. The goal of waiting on God in prayer is to know Him. He delights in revealing Himself to us if we will only make the time.

We may have many cares and worries foremost in our minds when we come to God in prayer. We may feel they need to be addressed, some urgently. But as we worship, wait, and meditate on Him, all our cares and worries fade away in view of His matchless presence. This is the reason it's so important not to rush into His presence talking about all our problems. God deeply cares about everything that bothers us, but what we need is not an answer. We need *The Answer!* He is the answer. Most of what we struggle with is a result of being distant from God. When we focus on our problems and the need, they become bigger. When we come close to Him, the opposite happens and the struggle ceases.

Be Still and Know That I Am God

Have you ever heard the statement, "The joy is in the journey"? This statement is never truer than in waiting on God. When we enter the secret place, thinking we'll get something from God and He'll do something for us, we miss the whole point. The reward is in the routine. Once the routine becomes a habit, we will find God's grace in it. Prayer is abiding and making our home in Him. It is to become as normal a practice for us as getting dressed every morning. When we develop the habit and establish the routine of our time with God, we feel completely naked and vulnerable to face the day without it. That feeling itself is a sweet reward in our spirit.

We live in a world pressuring us to arrive somewhere or accomplish something. We become goal oriented and many times unconsciously take this attitude into prayer. We pray to get something to happen right then. When our focus is on the reward of prayer, we will view the routine as an unpleasant necessity to get the reward. Yet *the joy has to be in the routine.* We must focus on abiding in Him, not on accomplishing something or arriving at a certain place in prayer. We will never do either of these until we abide. The key to life is not arriving or accomplishing, but abiding in someone. That someone is God. Joy and satisfaction come from abiding in Him. He is the reward.

David said in Psalm 73:26, *"My flesh and heart may fail; but God is the strength of my heart and my portion forever."* We don't draw near to God for Him to give us some portion. We draw near to receive Him as our portion. One of the definitions of the word *portion* is *the amount of food that is served to a person at one time.* We don't come to Him to get food. *He is our food!*

When we feast on His presence, we find Him as our provision—not our provider. Certainly, He does provide everything we need, but we seek His face, not His hand. We seek *Him,* not what He can do. Of course, God will answer our prayers and give us the breakthroughs we need. But I'm trying to get you to see that He alone is everything we need. He is the All-Sufficient One!

Until we learn to wait silently, patiently, before the Lord, we will always be worried about the cares of life and afraid of the future. When we spend time waiting on the Lord with childlike trust, worshipping Him for who He is, peace will invade our thoughts, assuring us that everything is going to be okay. We will rest in the fact that our life and future are in His hands. We will become confident that nothing the enemy throws against us will stop His will from coming to pass in our lives.

Is Your God Too Small?

How we see God when facing needs or difficulties determines everything else about us. Sadly, many of us have a view of Him that is too small. When our view of God is small, our problems will seem big. When we see Him as a big God, our problems will seem small. We need to constantly check ourselves to see if we have made God too small in our eyes. There is one sure way to keep that from happening.

We must always think and meditate about God this way: He is infinite and immeasurable. Before creation, all that existed was the Trinity: Father, Son and Holy Spirit. He was, and is everything. He doesn't exist in space and time. He made space and time; therefore, they exist in Him.

God is omnipresent. There's not a place where He is not present. God is omniscient. There's nothing He doesn't know. In fact, all knowledge exists in Him. God is omnipotent. He is all-powerful. There's no power or authority that did not come from Him. Men and governments seem so powerful to us, but they would have no power if God did not give it to them.

God is eternal. He has no beginning or end. He always existed and always will long after the earth is gone. To be anything less would make Him something less than God. What a glorious God we serve! He is bigger than our minds could ever begin to grasp. The fact that I can't fully describe Him doesn't make me doubt Him. It humbles me and inspires me to worship Him as God. We serve a great God!

A.W. Tozer writes:

> What comes into our minds when we think about God is the most important thing about us.... Worship is pure or base as the worshiper entertains high or low thoughts of God.
>
> For this reason the gravest question before the Church is always God Himself, and the most portentous fact about any man is not what he at a given time may say or do, but what he in his deep heart conceives God to be like. We tend by a secret law of the soul to move toward our mental image of God.....
>
> Were we able to extract from any man a complete answer to the question, "What comes into your mind when you think about God?" we might predict with certainty the spiritual future of that man....
>
> A right conception of God is basic not only to systematic theology but to practical Christian living as well. It is to worship what the foundation is to the temple; where it is inadequate or out of plumb the whole structure must sooner or later collapse. I believe there is scarcely an error in doctrine or a failure

in applying Christian ethics that cannot be traced finally to imperfect and ignoble thoughts about God....

The Lord of Hosts is with Us

Besides death, loneliness and rejection are the greatest fears we face as humans. We live in constant fear of having to live life alone. We also fear being rejected by those we care about. We live with these fears because we're looking for people to give us the security and sense of self-worth only found in God.

As we wait on Him daily in prayer, we will have an abiding confirmation that God is with us in the tough and even devastating places of our lives. We know the fact that He will never leave us nor forsake us as a theological truth, but for those who wait upon Him, it becomes a reality of our everyday experience. He becomes all we need in every situation.

Years ago, one of the men of our church walked into my office, sat down, and proceeded to tell me everything he felt was wrong with me as a pastor. After several hours of being judged and criticized, I walked out of my office and headed to my car to go home. I couldn't wait to get there. I knew my wife would be waiting for me, and she would console me and tell me how wrong this man was.

As I was leaving, I distinctly heard the Lord speak to me. He asked, "Where are you going?"

"I'm going home to my wife so she can encourage me," I said.

"Your wife can encourage you, but she can't heal you. Only I can heal you," He said.

Feeling reprimanded by His words, I immediately turned and went into the church auditorium. Even though I was all alone, I was keenly aware of the presence of Jesus there with me. I got on my knees and poured out all my hurt and insecurities before Him. When I finished, I felt the overwhelming sense of God's presence comforting me and pulling out all the darts of accusation that had lodged in my soul.

I cannot express what healing, cleansing, and comfort I experienced at that moment.

The room was filled with light. I discovered that in my darkest hour, God was with me. He was not only my Savior and Lord, but He was also my friend. I went home to my wife whole and filled with victory, instead of defeated and hurt.

We need good, healthy relationships in our lives, but it's important that we understand what people can and cannot give us. There are some things only God can give us. The world is full of insecure people who are looking for love and acceptance in all the wrong places. We want people to accept us so we can feel validated as a person, but we can only find that validation in God.

The fact that God designed and created us and paid the ultimate price of His Son's death to bring us back to Him is what gives us our identity. He wants us. He loves us. Nothing can separate us from His love, and that is what gives us our security. The revelation of this is awakened and becomes reality in us only as we spend time with God every day.

> He Himself has said, 'I will never leave you nor forsake you.' So we may boldly say: 'The Lord is my helper; I will not fear. What can man do to me?"
>
> Hebrews 13:5-6

This is a glorious truth! Once we grasp it, we will never feel lonely again. We will find friendship and comfort that no man or woman can ever give us. Insecurity and the desire for the approval of man will melt in the arms of Jesus as we are still and know He is God.

God is our Refuge

> I will say of the Lord, 'He is my refuge and my fortress; My God, in Him I will trust.' Surely He shall deliver you from the snare of the fowler and from the perilous pestilence. He shall

cover you with His feathers, And under His wings you shall take refuge; His truth shall be your shield and buckler.

Psalm 91:2-4

I want to ask you a question: Who or what do you first run to when danger or difficulty comes? What or who you run to reveals what or who you trust to protect you and deliver you. There are things we face in life that nobody can protect us from. One of the benefits of waiting on God in prayer is that He hides us securely in His presence.

God doesn't make a shelter for us; He becomes our shelter. When life throws its toughest circumstances our way, we find peace in the midst of the storm as we sit still in His presence. The situation around us may not change immediately, but we feel safe and protected in Him. We know we don't have to be afraid of anything that comes our way. We don't feel vulnerable and exposed to the opinions of man because we have found Him as our refuge. When life gets tough and we feel all alone, we run to Him.

When Saul pursued David many times to kill him, and when Absalom, his son, betrayed him and he had to run for his life, he penned an exuberant declaration of faith that we reference again from Psalm 27:1-6:

"The Lord is my light and my salvation; whom shall I fear? The Lord is the

strength of my life; of whom shall I be afraid? When the wicked came against me

to eat up my flesh, my enemies and foes, they stumbled and fell. Though an army

may encamp against me, my heart shall not fear; though war may rise against me,

in this will I be confident. One thing I have desired of the Lord, that will I seek:

that I may dwell in the house of the Lord all the days of my life, to behold the

beauty of the Lord, and to inquire in His temple. For in the time of trouble He

shall hide me in His pavilion; in the secret place of His tabernacle He shall hide

me; He shall set me high upon a rock. And now my head shall be lifted up above

my enemies all around me; Therefore I will offer sacrifices of joy in His

tabernacle; I will sing, yes, I will sing praises to the Lord....

When the Lord is our security, no matter what happens or who comes against us, we will not despair. For as we wait on Him and abide in His love in the midst of the raging storms of life, our hearts will also see above the storms, and we will sing.

Pruning

Why does my flesh dig in its heels, pulling on me to delay or
procrastinate spending time with You?

It really is a battle of will; my flesh does not want to sit still.
It wants to be active, pushing, driving,
accomplishing something it can see.

My heart longs for quietness and the overwhelming peace that
comes when I am with You.

I am not walking with You today.
I am sitting, rocking gently in my little swing,
watching all You have made live with carefree abandon.

I see that as a prize to press toward,
living with that same carefree abandon, knowing
You will take care of everything that concerns me.

I am looking at the Easter lilies I bought a couple of years ago.
After they bloomed, I planted them by my front door
to remind me of Your sacrifice as I pass by them on my way.

Easter is long past and they are just now blooming.
They were forced to bloom early
for the stores and now they are off of their natural schedule.

How often Lord, have I forced blooms in my life,
thinking I was ready to "take on" something before the time
and schedule that You had ordained?

I see my Spirea bushes that have bloomed so profusely. The
blooming bush was breathtaking!

But, now comes the part that is hard for me.
If it is to bloom again this season, then I must cut it back hard.
It won't even look like it had ever bloomed. If I don't cut it back,
energy that would be used to make new blossoms will be used
trying to nourish dead, dry blooms.

What a lesson!

Your Word says so plainly, "forgetting what lies behind
and pressing forward to the prize
of the mark of the upward call in Christ"

Every time I do something for You that would be considered to be a
blossom that others benefit from and enjoy, *of necessity*,
that very thing can't be allowed to remain as
a dead tribute to a past triumph or it will hinder or even stop me
from being able to repeat the bloom.

Oh, Lord, as much as I know how necessary this is,
because I am about to do the same to my bushes, I say to you,
"Lord, cut me back hard after every victory and triumph."

Cut off even in my own mind the thrill and memory of those things.
Let the beauty of my blossoming be a treasured memory in your
heart and let the lingering fragrance of things done with a pure
heart cause You to smile at the thought of them.

Let the cutting back bring me to full humility in the knowledge
that I can do nothing without You.

Above all, I do not want pride of past triumphs to stand out
in my life like spent, dried blossoms that are not capable
of producing anything beautiful again.

I lift my life to You, Lord. I trust You.
Your cutting back is not in the physical realm,
so I have no fear of calamity.

It is in my heart, my soul, and my mind.
I lift my heart to You in complete trust.
..........CUT!!!

Donna Shelton
6/8/00

Creating an Atmosphere of Worship

Worship is the gateway to the secret place. A large portion of our time in prayer should be spent worshipping God. In Matthew 6:9, the Lord's Prayer begins with "Our Father in heaven, hallowed be Your name." Our time in the secret place should always begin with a heart full of worship and thankfulness. There's no quicker and more effective way to fill the prayer room with the presence of God than this.

Psalm 22:3 says, *"You are holy, enthroned in the praises of Israel."* This is a powerful truth. Just picture the eternal God sitting down and making His habitation in the praises of His people. In the prayer room, there's nothing more to be desired than God's manifest presence. His presence will cure cold, dry praying.

During prayer, I've found it beneficial to spend time in worship at intervals along the way. When we pray for someone, we need to stop and worship Him. When we talk to God about our needs, we need to stop and worship Him. When God speaks to us through a scripture, we need to stop and worship Him. A heart of worship should never be far from our lips. (I say "a heart of worship" because even though God blesses us as we worship Him, we don't worship to get blessed. We worship Him simply to honor Him and give Him His rightful place.)

Jesus explained to the woman at the well that the Father seeks worshippers who will worship Him in spirit and truth (John 4:23). Our hearts must be fully engaged and full of gratitude. This is no dry, intellectual exercise. Our head will never take us there. True worship is a heart overflowing with passion for God and who He is, not just for what He gives us. Praise is reserved for that. You praise Him for all His blessings, but you worship Him for who He is.

Secondly, He wants those who will worship Him in truth. *Worship* means *to ascribe worth*. In order to truly worship Him, we need to know Him, His attributes, His character, and His nature. Don't let worship remain at the basic level of "God, I love You. I worship You. I honor You." What is it about Him that you love? Why do you honor Him? Tell Him! You have to know something about the details of His worth. Worship Him in the truth of who He is. As you do this, your heart will explode with the awesomeness of your great God!

Knowing God

Now acquaint yourself with Him, and be at peace. Thereby good will come to you.

Job 22:21

Jeremiah tells us not to glory in our own wisdom, might or riches. He tells us to glory in understanding and knowing God, which delights Him.

Thus says the Lord:

Let not the wise *man* glory in his wisdom,
Let not the mighty *man* glory in his might,
Nor let the rich *man* glory in his riches;
But let him who glories glory in this,

That he understands and knows Me,
That I *am* the Lord, exercising loving kindness,
judgment, and righteousness in the earth.
For in these I delight," says the Lord.

Jeremiah 9:23-2

Acquaint yourself with this God who exercises loving kindness, judgment, and righteousness. Seek to know something about each one of these attributes because each one is filled with a beauty and wonder all its own. Even God's judgment fills your heart with awe and wonder when you understand how righteous His judgment is.

God is perfect and right in all His ways. He is eternal, sovereign, holy, immutable, and supreme in His reign. He is infinite in His knowledge, His wisdom, His power, and His presence. He's a faithful God, filled with goodness and kindness. He is love, full of grace and mercy.

To whom then will you liken God? Or what likeness will you compare to Him?

Isaiah 40:12-18

Skeptics will say they can't believe in God because they can't wrap their mind around Him. Everything has to be filtered through their rational thoughts. But God is infinite and eternal. If we could grasp the ends of His nature and being with our natural mind, then we would be God. Only something or someone greater than us and beyond us can inspire true worship. The things about God that are beyond our understanding should not make us doubt Him. Rather, they should fill our hearts with an awe and wonder that causes us to bow down and worship Him.

For example, let's focus on an attribute we don't often think about, the solitariness of God. *The Attributes of God,* by Arthur W. Pink, has been of great help to me. The book includes a chapter on each of the many attributes of God. Let's look at an excerpt from Arthur Pink's book.

Who is like unto Thee, O Lord, among the gods? Who is like Thee, glorious in holiness, fearful in praises, doing wonders?" (Exodus 15:11). "In the beginning, God" (Genesis 1:1). There was a time; if "time" it could be called, when God, in the unity of His nature (though subsisting equally in three Divine Persons), dwelt all alone. There was no heaven, where His glory is now particularly manifested. There was no earth to engage His attention. There were no angels to sing His praises; no universe to be upheld by the word of His power. There was nothing, no one, but God; and that, not for a day, a year, or an age, but "from everlasting." During a past eternity, God was alone: self-contained, self-sufficient, self-satisfied; in need of nothing. If a universe, angels, or human beings been necessary to Him in any way, they also had been called into existence from all eternity. The creation of them added nothing to God essentially. "He changes not" (Malachi 3:6), therefore His essential glory can be neither augmented nor diminished.

Oh, how this thrills the heart and expands the mind! My mind cannot grasp existence from all eternity, but my heart leaps within me, and says, "Yes! My God is solitary in His existence and self-sufficiency." Knowing the limitations and weaknesses of my own existence, I fall on my knees and worship a solitary God who would love a mere mortal like me. Worship is not about us; it's about God. It's about spending time getting to know Him more intimately. This is the greatest activity a human being can engage in.

Giving God All the Glory

And whatever you do in word or deed, do all in the name of the Lord Jesus, giving thanks to God the Father through Him.

Colossians 3:17

In everything give thanks; for this is the will of God in Christ Jesus for you.

1 Thessalonians 5:18

True worship should evolve into thanksgiving and praise. We worship God for who He is, but we praise Him for what He does. Praise is equally as important as worship. Never forget to thank God for each thing He does for you. When you get your paycheck, thank Him. If you had a safe trip, thank Him. If you had an enjoyable time with a friend, thank Him. If you woke up this morning and had breath, thank Him! Take every little blessing as an opportunity to thank Him.

Paul says grace should cause "thanksgiving to abound to the glory of God" (2 Cor. 4:15). Praising and giving thanks to God is all about who gets the glory. The summary statement of the Westminster Catechism says, "The chief end of man is to glorify God and enjoy Him forever." This is the entire reason for our existence.

Every good gift and every perfect gift is from above, and comes down from the Father of lights, with whom there is no variation or shadow of turning.

James 1:17

Even if the blessing seems to come from man, God is still the source of the blessing. All the glory belongs to Him. This is not to be treated as some idea of being generally thankful to God. Paul said to give the glory to God for whatever we do in word or deed. We are to be very specific in giving God the glory for each blessing.

There is a spiritual law that I call the "cycle of glory." Grasping this truth will take a little effort, but it's worth the journey. In the Bible there are certain concepts we sometimes make out to be mystical and mysterious, when in reality they're to be applied in a practical way to our lives. I would suppose there's not one single word in the Bible that would fit that category more than the word *glory*. I pray that as I explain this law it will change the way you live just as it has changed me. There are two sides to this cycle of glory we need to understand.

1. The Glory of God

God and everything He does is full of glory. *Glory* is simply defined as the *weightiness of splendor*. If I were to say that a person is glorious, I would be referring to the splendor of their intelligence, strength, beauty, and accomplishments. Whatever attributes were ascribed to them—summed up—would be their splendor. *Weightiness of splendor* refers to the measure of it. Glory is not an attribute of God, but is the weight of splendor and majesty on any and all of His attributes. His wisdom, His power, and His love are all infinite in the weight of their splendor. Moses asked to see God's glory but was told he wouldn't live if he did. God did allow him to feel His Presence as He passed by, and he was given the tiniest of glimpse of His splendor.

In the secret place of prayer, God's glory is that unseen weightiness of His splendor that overwhelms us when His presence is near. When we give Him glory, He always shows up. There is no way to describe it. It's beyond our understanding, yet our hearts cry out for it.

In Revelation John tells us the Lord Almighty and the Lamb are the temple and that there's no more need for sun or moon, because the glory of God illuminates the holy city (Revelation 21:22-23). Think of the brightness of the noonday sun—gazing at it would blind you. The bright shining of the sun is its glory. Yet, the glory of the sun pales in comparison to the glory of the Lamb. When God answers a prayer, the answer is not our greatest gift. Our greatest gift is the glory of God that is on the answered prayer!

2. Giving God Glory

Declare His glory among the nations, His wonders among all peoples. For the Lord is great and greatly to be praised; He is also to be feared above all gods. For all the gods of the peoples are idols, But the Lord made the heavens. Honor and majesty are before Him; Strength and gladness are in His place. Give to the Lord, O families of the peoples, Give to the Lord glory and strength. Give to the Lord the glory due His name; Bring an offering, and come before Him. Oh, worship the Lord in the beauty of holiness!

1 Chronicles 16:24-29

We are to give God the glory due His name. How do we give something to God that already belongs to Him? Literally, in whatever we do, we're to stop and purposefully return the glory back to God (1 Cor. 10:31). He gives us breath. He gives us strength to work and play. Every meaningful relationship comes from Him. All of the possessions we enjoy come from Him. Every blessing we receive comes from Him. We should constantly be giving the glory back to Him.

As a spiritual exercise, take one week and commit yourself to do this continually. Thank Him for everything saying, "God, You have blessed me. I get to enjoy this blessing, but I don't want to keep the glory. I give the glory back to You." I guarantee when you do this, God's presence will begin to permeate the very atmosphere of your life. This more than anything turns talking with God into walking with God. Returning the glory to Him brings God into every detail of your life. This is what a life of prayer is all about!

Everything Has Glory on It

Everything God has made has glory on it (1 Corinthians 15:39-41). The sun, the moon, and the stars all have glory. The reason we can sit in awe as we watch a sunset is because it's glorious. Why are we inspired watching an eagle fly or a horse run? It's because they are creatures God has made, and they have glory on them. We as humans also have glory on us.

What is man that You are mindful of him, And the son of man that You visit him? For You have made him a little lower than the angels, And You have crowned him with glory and honor.

Psalm 8:4-5

Since God has crowned us with glory, everything we produce has glory on it. For example, when we watch something like the Olympic Games and see the best athletes in the world compete, we're seeing the glory of God on them. Our hearts are filled with joy when we watch someone graduate from college because we're seeing the glory of God. When we listen to Beethoven's Symphony no. 5 or view Van Gogh's *Starry Night,* we're getting a taste of the glory of God. These men may not even believe in Him, but their genius is a gift of God's glory. All of this glory belongs to God and Him alone. We get to enjoy these many blessings, but we're not supposed to keep any of the glory.

False Glory

We should live recognizing and acknowledging God's glory in all things. When we don't, we proceed to try to create our own glory. This is a false glory. It's why people go to nightclubs. They don't realize what they're feeling is the absence of God's glory, so they go where loud music is playing, lights are flashing, and drinks are being poured. They mingle with people they've never met and think it's so exciting! They think this is glorious and fun. At 5:00 a.m., when the music and lights are gone, the place is empty, and the 60-watt bulbs in the ceiling come on it reveals that it was all a lie. The place is a dump and rats are running around the room. They wake up the next morning with a hangover and with someone they don't remember. It's all just false glory.

Why do people seek such things that never really satisfy? It's because we were all made to enjoy things that have God's glory on them. We will then have glory to give back to God in thankfulness. This is the cycle of glory. We seek God, and in turn, He blesses us. We enjoy the blessing, but return the glory to Him in thanksgiving and gratefulness. Only as we give the glory back to Him does He continue to pour out His blessings on us. When we keep the blessing and the glory without returning it to Him from our hearts, we stop the cycle of God's blessing.

There's a story in the gospels where Jesus heals ten lepers. All of them were healed, yet only one of them returned to give God the glory for his healing (Luke 17:15-19). I'm sure the other nine thought it wasn't that big of a deal to return the glory to God. But the one who returned and gave the glory to God received something the others didn't. He was made whole!

Do you understand how significant this was? All ten lepers had lost toes, fingers, and probably parts of their noses to this horrible disease. When they were healed, it meant the leprosy was gone, but they were still missing body parts. But the one who returned the glory to God was made *completely whole!* So even though all of them were healed, only one was not left crippled by the past of his disease.

How many Christians have been healed, but are still not whole because they didn't give the glory to God? Dear friends, God has been so good to us, yet we miss out on so much more that God would do if we would just be faithful to thank Him and give Him all the glory.

A Jealous God

I don't think many Christians understand how strongly God feels about returning glory to Him. He is a jealous God. He will not give His glory to another (Isaiah 42:8). He does not allow another to keep His glory. The question is this: Why?

A popular American TV star once relayed how she gave up her belief in God. She was raised in church, but as a young woman, she heard her pastor preach a sermon on how God was jealous for our love. She said that did it for her. She began to wonder, *How can a God who is supposed to be the infinite creator of all things be jealous of me?* But God never said He was jealous *of* us, He said He was jealous *for* us.

There's a big difference between being jealous *of* someone and being jealous *for* someone. We become jealous of each other because the other person has something we don't, and we want it. But God is jealous for us because He has something we don't have, and He wants to give it to us! He knows that He designed us for Himself. Our lives only become full and complete when we remain in close fellowship with Him. When we stray from Him, it robs His heart of the privilege of blessing us. In other words, He's not jealous because He needs something; He's jealous because *we need* something.

C.S. Lewis wrestled with this idea. He was bothered when reading things like Ephesians 1:6, 12, 14 where it says God performs all His acts that we might praise Him and give Him glory. Lewis said he never noticed until then that all enjoyment overflows spontaneously into praise. We praise what we value. When God does something for us, praise completes the enjoyment of the experience.

Look at it this way. When a boy finds a new love, it's not enough for him to just enjoy the relationship. He has to praise her to everyone, friends and strangers alike. Telling everyone how wonderful she is completes the enjoyment of the relationship. When we do the same with God, not only telling Him how wonderful He is and all that He has done but telling anyone who will listen, it completes us and makes us whole.

Giving You Glory

Oh, how I love our special place
Where we commune together, face to face
Over my head a canopy of blue
White clouds floating by, fashioned by You

Breezes whisper their own gentle song
Caressing my face as they journey on
Birds and insects continually sing
A song of praise to their Creator and King

Enthralled with the beauty of Your creation
I lift my life in complete adoration
I'm filled with such wonder at all you do
Yet, I'm not afraid to be friends with You

Creator, my God, my Father, my King
Of all You've created, I'm one little being
So grateful my heart and thankful am I
If I could not praise You, I know I would die

Donna Shelton
2/19/96

The Voice of God

God is not just a God who speaks; He is a speaking God. Everything in the world happens by God speaking. The second person of the godhead is the Word (John 1:1). When God decided to create in the beginning, He spoke, and it happened. The Spirit was hovering over the vast darkness, maybe for a million or billion years, waiting to act, but nothing happened until the Word was heard speaking. He said, "Let there be light," and there was light (Genesis 1:1-3).

When God speaks, hell trembles, and heaven stands at attention. Angels are dispatched when He speaks. At God's voice, the Red Sea parted, Daniel was kept safe in the lion's den, the three Hebrew men weren't burned in the fiery furnace, and Elijah was fed by ravens in a time of famine. When Jesus spoke, the sick were healed, demons were cast out, blind eyes were opened, and deaf ears were unstopped. When He spoke to the storm, it had no choice but to be still. Nothing is impossible when God speaks.

Oh, how we need to hear the voice of God, yet there are many people who say that He doesn't speak to us today. They say God quit speaking when the last apostle died. Because we now have the written Word, they say God only speaks through its pages. Yet this makes no sense at all. Why? Because if God is not still speaking, the Bible would just be ink on paper. The written words themselves don't talk. We need the Holy Spirit to speak to us so those words on the page can become *rhema* or the living Word to us.

Has God been silent since the book of Acts? No! Has Jesus, the Word, been removed from the godhead? No! Before Jesus ascended to heaven, He told the disciples that He would send another Helper, the Holy Spirit, one just like Himself. Is the Holy Spirit mute? No! Is something wrong with Him that He doesn't speak today? No! Did He go silent after the last apostle? No!

One of the most important secrets of the secret place is the secret of hearing the voice of God. What joy His voice has brought me in times of trouble! What comfort it has brought me in times of loss, and what peace it has brought me in times of making big decisions!

The only reason I refer to hearing God's voice as a secret is because so many Christians have told me they've never heard the voice of God. Christians don't hear the voice of God speaking to them personally for one of two reasons: either they aren't listening, or they just don't know how to recognize His voice. It's not because He's not talking to them.

I'm reminded of a talkative young pastor. Since one of my roles in ministry is mentoring pastors, my wife and I sat with a young pastor and his wife a while back who had been in the ministry only a few years. The young pastor talked non-stop the entire time we were together. I could hardly get in a few sentences. Afterward, I said to my wife, "I've been in the ministry for forty years. I've pastored two churches for most of that time. Doesn't he realize I probably know a few things that would help him if he would only ask?" He walked away from that meeting no wiser than when he walked in.

This is the way many people pray even though prayer should be a dialogue. Prayer should be two people meeting together for a conversation. One of the greatest hindrances to prayer is when we do all the talking, thinking God is just there to listen. In prayer we're sitting before the Creator of the Universe! He has all wisdom. He knows everything we need to know yet we often talk the whole time. Yes, God loves to hear what's on our minds. But we need to hear Him talk more than He needs to hear us talk! This requires something many of us are not good at—*listening!*

When our boys were still children, I would tell them to do something. Later, when I asked them if it was done, they would say they didn't hear me tell them to do it. I said, "No, you heard me, but you weren't listening."

Do you have an ear to hear what the Spirit is saying (Revelation 2:29)? I know you have ears, but are you listening? Just because you sat silently for a few moments at the end of your prayer time, waiting to see if God wanted to say something doesn't mean you were listening. First of all, God doesn't speak on command. God doesn't speak just because you say, "Ok, God, it's Your turn. I've got five minutes, so let's hear it. Speak." You will seldom hear God speak this way. Why? It's because you're telling God when to speak. He will not speak to you on your terms, but on His. You are not in charge of the conversation.

Listening is more about our posture toward God. It requires a surrendered heart. We need to begin our prayer time by saying, "God, how do You want this prayer time to go today?" He may keep us focused on one verse during our reading of the Scriptures. If He does, then stop, listen, and say, "God, what do You want to speak to me from this?"

In the midst of worship, you may feel a strong sense of His presence. Don't move on. Sit in His presence. Bask in it. This is God speaking, affirming His love for you. As you're praying, you may begin to feel a strong burden or compassion for a person you know. This is probably God telling you to pray for them. If you have a list of people you want to pray for but feel a stronger burden when you get to a certain one, spend more time praying for that person. You always do your best praying when your spirit is moved to pray.

If you don't get to all the people on your list, don't worry about it. God may have laid that person on someone else's heart that day.

If you're watching the news and feel deep compassion or concern for something you hear, this is God asking you to lift that situation to Him. Be sensitive to the Spirit throughout the day. Look for God to speak to you. He speaks to those who are listening.

You may be driving and a thought comes to you. Stop and give that thought attention. Don't just pass it off. This could be God speaking. You'll never know unless you listen. God speaks on His own terms. If you cultivate a hearing ear, you'll gradually hear the voice of God more and more. Now that you're listening for His voice, how do you recognize Him when He speaks?

As a pastor, one of the most frequent questions I've been asked is, "How do you hear God's voice?" Recognizing the voice of God cannot be explained in a definitive set of principles. There are, however, a few tips I want to give you to help you.

It's interesting that when Jesus wanted to teach us about hearing His voice, He used the analogy of sheep. He said the sheep know His voice because they follow Him. Sheep follow their shepherd until his voice becomes easily recognizable to them.

But he who enters by the door is the shepherd of the sheep. To him the doorkeeper opens, and the sheep hear his voice; and he calls his own sheep by name and leads them out. And when he brings out his own sheep, he goes before them; and the sheep follow him, for they know his voice. Yet they will by no means follow a stranger, but will flee from him, for they do not know the voice of strangers.

John 10:2-5

We learn to recognize God's voice the same way we learn to recognize anyone else's. We follow the person. We spend time listening to their voice. For instance, if my wife's voice was put with a thousand others, I could easily recognize it because I've spent lots of time listening to her. If I've known someone a short time, I would still probably be able to recognize his or her voice. It may be a little more difficult, and I may have to let the individual talk for a while before I figure out who he or she is. If I just met a man yesterday, I probably wouldn't recognize his voice until the man identified himself to me. It's the same way when we are learning to recognize God's voice. The more we listen to His voice, the more we will be able to recognize it.

Jesus said His sheep know His voice. This is a promise. We can know the voice of God because He promised we could. People struggling to know the voice of God are afraid it might be the devil talking to them. Jesus said we would know the difference. If our heart is humble before God, our Shepherd will not allow us to be deceived. The key is to stay humble and teachable.

It's very difficult to hear the voice of God when we approach Him from fear. Fear has no place in the throne room. Satan will try to deceive us. He dresses up as an angel of light, but we have a great safeguard against deception, the written Word of God.

We'll address the importance of the written Word in prayer in a moment, but I need to make a key point here. Always have your Bible with you when you pray because when God speaks, it will always agree with the entirety of His written Word. God is never going to give you a revelation or tell you to do something that is contrary to His Word. If you believe God is speaking to you, check your Bible to see if it agrees with what you've heard. If it doesn't, immediately throw out what you thought you heard and renounce any acceptance or association with it. Make this a demonstrative act. Let the enemy know you will not put up with his deception.

If what you heard agrees with the written Word, joyously thank the Lord for speaking to you. Don't be casual about it. You have just heard the voice of the infinite Creator of all things! Thankfulness and praise always water and cultivate any activity of the Holy Spirit.

Obviously, the Word doesn't specifically mention everything God speaks to you. For instance, God may impress upon you to speak to your next-door neighbor about the condition of his or her soul. You won't find a verse that says, "Go talk to your next-door neighbor tomorrow morning." You will find that what He told you is consistent with the commands in scripture. Jesus said in Mark 16:15 to *"go into all the world and preach the gospel to every creature.*" Your neighbor is a creature, and you are a "goer."

The devil will never tell you to do something that lines up with the truths and principles of scripture. If you hear a voice telling you to cut off someone who has hurt you, you can be sure it's not God's voice. Luke 6 tells you to love your enemies and do good to those who hate you. Once you understand the principles that govern hearing the voice of God, it really becomes quite easy.

Satan is called the deceiver because he lies. Just as God is constantly speaking to us, the devil is also trying to speak to us. It's easy to know when he is talking. He lies! In fact, the devil can't tell the truth because there's no truth in him (John 8:44). He couldn't tell the truth if tried.

The enemy is constantly trying to sow thoughts in our minds. The narrative goes something like this. The devil will say, "God doesn't really love you. He's not hearing your prayers. You're no good. You'll never get out of this mess. There's no hope for you." These are all lies! Just check the Scriptures. The devil is always a liar, but our God is not a man that He should lie. When God says it, He will do it!

The Sound of His Voice

God speaks in many ways. He speaks through dreams, visions, His audible voice, the prophetic, and, of course, through His written Word. All of these are important, but the most common way God speaks to us is through what many call the "inward witness." This is the most important one in prayer and, in fact, in our daily lives.

The Spirit Himself bears witness with our spirit that we are children of God.

Romans 8:16

God's voice is in us, and He's speaking all the time. If we don't know how to recognize His voice, we probably think He's not speaking to us. But He is! This is one of the most important reasons God has given the Holy Spirit to live in us. He is called the Spirit of truth.

But the Helper, the Holy Spirit, whom the Father will send in My name, He will teach you all things, and bring to your remembrance all things that I said to you.

John 14:26

So, how do we recognize the sound of God's voice? Does it have a sound? The answer is yes, but it's not the kind of sound you may think. In all things, God has created the natural world after the pattern of the spiritual world. In hearing the voice of God, we're not receiving natural knowledge. We're receiving spiritual knowledge. It's a spiritual activity, and remember, the natural man cannot receive the things of the Spirit of God.

For purposes of analogy, let's say when God speaks there are spiritual vibrations. In the natural, there aren't words floating out in the air, but vibrations created from a source of energy. So, most of the time when God speaks to us, it doesn't sound like complete words and sentences. It sounds like a vibe or vibration.

There are many wrong vibes out there today, so let's be clear we're talking about the voice of the Holy God. If we're only looking for words or sentences, we'll miss the voice of God in our spirits. We can feel a vibration. You may ask, "What does that vibe feel like?" Some of the words I would use to describe a vibe are a hunch, an intuition, a stop sign, an illumination, a heaviness, or a lightness. Usually when we experience any of these things, we say, "I just *felt like* God was saying something."

Many times, when we feel these things, we shrug them off or think, *It was probably just me.* It may be just you, but it may not be just you. The Bible tells us to test the spirits to see if they are God. We will never begin to hear the voice of God until we start testing these feelings or witnesses to see if they are from our spirit, instead of our head or emotions.

For example, let's say you have a feeling or a hunch that you should take a different route to work today. It's just a fleeting notion. Who knows what trouble or danger God is trying to spare you? When we're learning to hear God's voice, we often look for His peace.

> **And let the peace (soul harmony which comes) from Christ rule (act as umpire continually) in your hearts [deciding and settling with finality all questions that arise in your minds, in that peaceful state] to which as [members of Christ's] one body you were also called [to live]. And be thankful (appreciative), [giving praise to God always].**
>
> **Colossians 3:15, AMP**

I love this verse, and it has been the deciding factor in many difficult decisions. God is a God of peace. If He's in it, you will feel peace. Paul said peace acts as an umpire in your spirit, deciding and settling all questions. Do you have a question? Ask peace. Do you have a decision to make? Let peace decide. Do you have an issue that needs to be settled? Let peace settle it.

Isn't it wonderful that you have an umpire inside of you? If you want to please God and win at the game of life, listen to the umpire. Stop arguing with Him, thinking He made the wrong call. He knows more about the rules of this game than you do.

One of the greatest lessons in life is if we don't have peace about something, we don't do it until or unless peace comes! How many troubles and heartaches have we endured because we wanted something so badly we went ahead with it even though we didn't have peace?

My Greatest Lesson

When I was twenty-four years old I had a vision. In this vision I saw myself preaching to thousands of people. The Lord said, "This is a church I want you to start in St. Louis. If you will be faithful and obedient to Me, what you see in this vision will come to pass." This vision was a life-changing experience for me.

With the vision, I sensed God was leading me to go back to school for a year before launching this church. I ended up at a Bible college in Dallas, Texas. Near the end of my time there, a local pastor of a very large church offered me a job as his associate pastor. A few days later, I received the same offer from another pastor of a leading church in the city. Both of these were tremendous opportunities. I would be ministering to thousands of people. My family would be well taken care of financially. Most twenty-five year olds would jump at a chance like this, and I must say I was very much enticed. There was just one problem—this vision thing.

Visions, like any experience, have a way of growing dim after a while. I was starting to doubt the vision and began to think, *Did God really speak to me? How can I know for sure I'm supposed to do this now?* The two opportunities in Dallas were a sure thing. Back in St. Louis, there was nothing; it was only a dream. How could I pass up these opportunities? I was undecided on what to do.

For days, it was all I could think about. I pondered all the pros and cons of each opportunity offered to me. The more I thought about it, the more confused I became. I didn't know what to do. I wondered how I could ever know what the will of God was.

Finally, I decided to meet with the second pastor who made me the offer, and I laid out my dilemma before him. I knew he was a wise, seasoned pastor and would give me good advice. His counsel not only helped me to find God's will in this situation, but it also gave me valuable insight for hearing the voice of God for the rest of my life.

"Rick," he said, "You have three ways to go, right? Only one of them can be the path God wants you to take." This all seemed obvious. I didn't see how this was getting me any closer to knowing God's will for my life. Then he made the statement that changed everything. He said, "Forget all the pros and cons of each opportunity. What is in your heart? That is God's will for you." While he said this, he placed his hand on his chest.

Then, pointing to his head, he said, "The two that are not God's will are in your head. God leads us through peace. When you find that peace, it lights up your spirit. It's like the sun shining in your soul. When your mind runs wild, thinking about all the pros and cons of each opportunity, your head is active; creating a cloud of confusion that blocks the light of peace from shining in your heart. You need to shut down your mind. Stop working so hard trying to figure this thing out. Get alone with God, sit at His feet, and worship Him. If you will do this, the cloud of thoughts in your mind will dissipate, and the peace of God will come shining through."

Armed with this wisdom, I closed myself in with God. I decided that for the next few days I was not going to think about my decision at all. I was just going to sit at the feet of Jesus until the cloud broke up and peace started shining through. To be honest, I thought it would probably take a few days before this happened. But once my mind quieted down, almost immediately I had my answer.

Deep down in my soul, all I could see was the vision God had given me a year earlier. Suddenly, the other two opportunities had no appeal to me whatsoever. I closed those doors, and soon I headed to St. Louis, Missouri, with my young wife and son to plant a new church.

What's interesting is that this option was by far the least appealing to my natural mind, but I was no longer listening to my head. I left with everything I owned in the back of my car, and I was the happiest man on earth. I had peace because I had allowed peace—not my head—to act as umpire, deciding and settling with finality all questions that arose in my mind.

I sit here many years later, thinking about the consequences of that decision. A church of thousands was raised up that sent out ministers all around the world. What would have happened if I had listened to my head, instead of following peace?

Dear friends, don't let money, security, or personal advantages be your deciding factor in any decision. These are all in your head. God's peace doesn't dwell there. Let the peace of God decide what's best for you. Not only will you fulfill God's plan for your life, but you will also be the happiest person on earth!

Soul Harmony

Peace is soul harmony. Peace is the sound of the voice of God. When you have peace, your soul is in complete harmony with the Spirit of God and the Word of God (Hebrews 12:14).

Don't ever override the voice of peace. When you do, a sense of misalignment comes inside your heart, and you will feel a disconnect between you and God. Many people want God to speak to them, but all the while they disregard His peace. They end up frustrated, condemned, and confused. These are all manifestations of disharmony. Many don't hear the voice of God because they're looking for the wrong thing. They are looking for a "word" when God is trying to give them a word through peace.

Overriding peace causes our heart to condemn us (1 John 3:21-22). This causes great difficulty in approaching God. He loves us and wants to spend time with us, but because we have violated peace, inside we feel judged and guilty. We feel like something is wrong with us. We have lost confidence in our standing before God.

We will never hear God's voice in this condition. Don't try to press on in prayer in the state of condemnation. Go back, repent, and get back into peace. Then the heavens will be open to you, God's presence will be near, and His voice will be clear.

One of the things that rob us of peace is when we want God to talk to us about something that *interests us.* This is trying to manipulate God. Instead, we need to find out what He's interested in and let Him talk to us about that. There are so many things we don't know about our situation or what we really need! We may be asking God to speak to us about our marriage when God wants to talk to us about our attitude.

Delight yourself also in the Lord, And He shall give you the desires of your heart.

Psalm 37:4

God gives the desires of the heart to those who delight themselves in Him. When we enter the prayer room with a list of all the things *we* desire, we end up with many unanswered prayers.

We come into the secret place to have sweet fellowship with the Father. We bought this field of prayer so we can find the treasure of His presence. We come to know Him and hear His heart. Then something unexpected happens to us. In the original language, "He shall give you the desires of your heart" actually says, "He shall assign to or create in you the desires of your heart." Therefore, as you delight yourself in the Lord, your desires change. The things you once thought you wanted are not so important to you any longer, because God has purified your desires. You are following the voice of peace. Once your desires are aligned with His will, whatever you ask, you will receive from Him.

Testing the Voice of God

When listening for the voice of God, we will seldom be 100% sure we have heard correctly. There are several voices that vie for our attention. There is the voice of reason, the voice of our emotions, and even the voice of our body speaking to us. Family and friends give us their opinion. There is the voice of the world around us and the voice of the devil. Especially when it comes from the voice of our own reasoning and emotions, it may sometimes be difficult to distinguish these from the voice of God. So, how do we know for sure when it's God is speaking?

> **Your own ears will hear him. Right behind you a voice will say, 'This is the way you should go,' whether to the right or to the left.**

> **Isaiah 30:21, NLT**

I find an important tip in this beautiful little verse. God rarely stands in front of us, speaking to us. When someone stands in front of us, we can easily hear what they are saying. It even makes it easier because we can see their lips forming the words. But when someone stands behind us, it is much more difficult.

It makes it even harder when He speaks in a still small voice as He did with Elijah, and this is usually the case. Why does God do this and speak softly? I believe it's because the exercise of hearing God's voice is not just about getting a word, but it's more about drawing close to God.

If someone is behind you speaking, it's nearly impossible to hear what they are saying while you are walking. But if you stand still, you can easily hear them (Psalm 46:10). If God were to stand in front of us, we could go on with all our busyness and activity and still hear Him. But He desires our undivided attention. We don't just need a word; we need Him. When we get Him, we get His voice.

Let's say that we hear a word: "This is the way, walk in it," but we're not 100% sure we've heard correctly. We might think God is saying, "Turn to the right," so we take a step in that direction. If we've heard correctly, we will feel more peace. If we've heard incorrectly, we will feel less peace.

I've practiced this for years, and it has proven to be an effective test of the voice of God. You might say, "But why would God use this trial and error method? Isn't it risky?" Again, God's ultimate purpose is not just to get a word to us but also to get us to learn to follow Him more closely. This method requires complete dependency upon Him. We have to follow Him closely every step of the way.

One of the greatest examples of this trial and error method is when the great apostle Paul was on one of his missionary journeys. He experienced tremendous success until they headed for Asia.

Now when they had gone through Phrygia and the region of Galatia, they were forbidden by the Holy Spirit to preach the word in Asia. After they had come to Mysia, they tried to go into Bithynia, but the Spirit did not permit them. So passing by Mysia, they came down to Troas. And a vision appeared to Paul in the night. A man of Macedonia stood and pleaded with him, saying, "Come over to Macedonia and help us."

Now after he had seen the vision, immediately we sought to go to Macedonia, concluding that the Lord had called us to preach the gospel to them.

Acts 16:6-10

Paul "felt" like the next place they ought to preach the gospel was Asia. But when he arrived, the Holy Spirit forbid him to preach there. What did "being forbidden" feel like to Paul? Maybe a stop sign, a "no" in his spirit, heaviness, or a general lack of peace? Whatever it was, Paul knew he was not supposed to stay there.

Then Paul "tried" to go to Bithynia. I love this word "tried." It demonstrates to us that Paul was experimenting in hearing the voice of God. He was not 100% sure this was where he was supposed to go, but he knew his heart was right and this was the best hunch he had at the moment. But again, the Spirit did not permit them. So, he headed through Mysia and ended up at Troas.

Probably at that point, Paul wasn't totally sure this was where God wanted him. What was interesting was that Troas actually appeared to be a dead end. He was staring at the Mediterranean Sea in front of him. If it would have been me, I would have been tempted to think, *Do I really know how to hear God's voice at all?* But at that moment, a vision appeared to Paul in the night. A man of Macedonia stood and pleaded with him to come to them. Macedonia was across the Mediterranean, so immediately Paul made plans to go to there.

I love the next statement that says they concluded that the Lord had called them to preach the gospel to the people of Macedonia. As a result of this trial and error exercise, all of Europe was opened up to the gospel. If Paul had waited back at home until he got a definitive word, he would have missed out on the biggest opportunity of his ministry up until that time. All of Europe would have been lost! I love the fact that through his hit-and-miss journey, Paul never once doubted that the Spirit had led him.

So many Christians sit at home waiting for a booming voice out of heaven that will give them 100% assurance they have heard the voice of God. I challenge you today to get up and go! Do what's in your heart. It may be a faint voice that seems uncertain, but if your heart is right and you stay close to Jesus, you will not fail. God will cover your mistakes. Hearing the voice of God is an act of faith. God will not judge you for missing it when you are honestly trying to obey His voice, but He will judge you for sitting at home doing nothing because you didn't receive an open vision.

My Journey

After God gave me the open vision, He told me to go back to school for a year. I felt I knew which school the Lord wanted me to attend. It was in Tulsa, Oklahoma. I was in Bennetsville, South Carolina so I packed up all our belongings in a U-Haul truck and headed cross-country to Tulsa.

School was about to start in a few days, but my wife was about to deliver our second child. I dropped her off in St. Louis to be with my parents while I went on to Tulsa to begin school. The first day I arrived, I unloaded our furniture into our apartment. The next day, I started school. When I walked in, the entire student body was gathered for a worship service. Everyone was praising God, and the room was filled with excitement, but there was a problem.

When I walked into the school, I felt a heaviness in my spirit. My joy and peace were gone. I knew the problem couldn't be the school. It was a wonderful place. I quickly realized the problem. I had missed God. God was "forbidding" me to stay there. I realized I was out of the will of God but what was I to do at that point? I had spent a great deal of money to get here. I knew in my heart that no matter what the cost, I had to find God's will.

I called my wife and said, "Guess what? I have missed God's voice. God doesn't want me here."

She said, "Well then, where does He want us?"

All I can say is, "Thank God I have a wife who treasures the will of God as much as I do!"

I said, "I'm not sure, but there's a new small school that was started by a church in Dallas, Texas. I feel that I should go and check it out." I got in my car and drove straight there. When I walked in the door of the school, which was being housed in the church auditorium, I felt the peace of God fill my being. The heaviness was gone. I knew this is where we were supposed to be.

After I had been in the school for about two weeks, an elderly woman who I didn't know walked up to me and said, "You're a pastor, aren't you?"

Somewhat taken aback, I replied, "Well, I was until I came here."

She proceeded, "Yes, and you pastored a church far away on the other side of the nation." Now, she had my attention. She said, "You have a wife and two sons." By this time, my wife had given birth to my second son.

"How did you know these things?" I responded.

"I am an intercessor," she said. "Earlier in the year, the Lord gave me a vision. I saw a pastor, his wife, and two sons. The Holy Spirit said to me, 'I want this pastor here in this school. I'm giving you the assignment of praying him to this place.'"

I guess God knew I needed lots of help in finding His will. I laughed and said, 'You're the reason I was so miserable at that school in Tulsa." Since that time, I've had tremendous respect for intercessors.

The blessings received and the lessons learned that year are so numerous I haven't enough room here to tell you about all of them. But a couple weeks later, in the beginning of a church service, the pastor walked up to me and said, "You're a pastor, aren't you?" I thought, *Here we go again!*

"The Lord just told me that I am supposed to take you under my wing, and we are going to become good friends," he said. I was thrilled! The things I learned from that pastor were far greater than what I learned in my classes. Now I knew why God wanted me here and nowhere else.

Do you see the great rewards of stepping out in faith on what little you hear? You may make some mistakes, but God has people you don't even know praying for you. Don't be afraid to fail. If you stay humble before God and keep your motives pure, He will protect you. The difference between those who hear the voice of God and those who don't is the one who hears, steps out in faith, fails, and gets up again while the other doesn't try at all because he's afraid of missing it.

A Right Heart

I've mentioned the importance of having a right heart many times already, but let me explain why this is so important in hearing the voice of God. When I asked my wife to marry me, as I described earlier, she said she loved me but she couldn't marry me. When I asked why, she said it was because I had said I would never be a pastor. She explained that when she was fourteen years old, God told her that's who she would marry. I told her I loved her too, but that I was never going to be a preacher so we broke off our relationship.

For nine weeks she prayed, asking God to speak to her because she was confused. She knew what God had spoken to her, but she also knew she had fallen in love with me. How could these two be reconciled? For nine weeks, God said nothing.

Finally, she said, "God, Your will is more important to me than anything else in the world. I don't just want to be in the center of Your will, I want to be in the center *of the center* of Your will." Still, God said nothing.

After all those weeks of praying and hearing nothing she told God that all she knew to do was follow her heart. Her heart was to marry me. She said, "God, at any step of the way, if You want to stop me, I will turn and run from him. Even the day of our wedding, as she was coming down the aisle, she said, "God, You still have time. Just say the word, and I'll run." Boy, am I glad God didn't stop her!

How could she do this knowing that it seemed contradictory to what God had spoken to her previously? First of all, we don't have all the pieces of the puzzle to our lives. God has a plan for our lives, He knows the future, and only He knows how it's all going to work out.

We know that all things work together for good to those who love God, to those who are the called according to His purpose.

Romans 8:28

During this time in my life, I was running from God and doing my own thing. I would not have been given this same freedom to trust my heart because my heart was not completely surrendered to Him. So much of success in the secret place is found in completely surrendering our will to His, then following our heart. The Holy Spirit will lead us through little nudges, thoughts, or just a feeling. Follow wherever the surrendered heart leads!

How could my wife be so bold as to say that she was going to follow her heart unless God stopped her? I've learned a great lesson down through the years: God gives great latitude to believers to follow their heart when it's completely surrendered to Him. Here is the lesson. If God does speak, we must obey. When He is silent, we can trust our heart if it is completely surrendered into His hands. My wife and I have now been in the ministry for over forty years. God definitely knew what He was doing!

Hearing God Through His Written Word

It's impossible to overemphasize the importance of our Bible in the secret place. It's our prayer book. When the fire of our prayer life seems to run out of fuel, we must find it again in the written Word of God. When we have nothing to say, we need to go to the Bible to give us new language to express our heart to Him. If we are not very proficient in the Word yet, we can just go to the Psalms and let the psalmist's prayers and songs be ours.

There are seventy-two prayers in the book of Psalms and two hundred twenty-two prayers in the Bible. We can take almost any passage in the Bible and turn it into a prayer by focusing on a truth, word, or

122

phrase that touches our heart. Meditation is the key to hearing God's voice through His written word.

> **This Book of the Law shall not depart from your mouth, but you shall meditate in it day and night, that you may observe to do according to all that is written in it. For then you will make your way prosperous, and then you will have good success.**
>
> Joshua 1:8

We're told to meditate in the Word day and night. We can easily be led astray in hearing God's voice when we don't spend time meditating on God's Word. Second Peter 1:19-20 calls scripture our prophetic Word confirmed. Our anchor and safeguard in hearing the voice of God is the written Word of God.

How we view the Bible will determine how we hear God speaking to us through it. The Bible is not a book of religion. Jesus never intended to start a religion. The Bible is not just a history book, although all of its history is true. It's called the gospel. The word *gospel* means *good news*. History is what happened in the past. News is what's happening today. The Bible, therefore, is not just a record of what God said. It's what God is saying to us today.

When you read the Bible, let God speak to you through it. The Bible is alive. It's different than any other book because it lives and breathes and is still speaking to us.

> **All Scripture is given by inspiration of God, and is profitable for doctrine, for reproof, for correction, for instruction in righteousness, that the man of God may be complete, thoroughly equipped for every good work.**
>
> 2 Timothy 3:16-17

The word *inspiration* in this verse means *God breathed.* God breathed upon people, and they wrote what they saw and heard. God's Word has His life and breath in it.

Paul prayed in Ephesians 1 that God's people would be given a spirit of wisdom and revelation in the knowledge of Jesus Christ.

Revelation describes what happens when God's written Word speaks to us. It means *to uncover* or *to see again*. Notice it doesn't say just to see, but it says to see again. What does this mean?

When God breathed on men of old, the Holy Spirit caused them to see things and then they wrote what they saw. When we get revelation, the same Holy Spirit that breathed on them breathes on us, and we see again what they saw originally. Do you see how powerful this is? The One who wrote the Bible is in us, and He speaks to us the same things in the same way that He spoke to them.

People often wonder what it must have felt like to be one of these men who had the Holy Spirit breathe on them and speak to them. I'm convinced we can know. When we meditate on the Scriptures and ask the Holy Spirit to reveal His truth to us, we'll find out. For instance, sometimes the Holy Spirit will open a scripture to me, and I'll jump up and shout, "Praise God! I see it! I get it!" His Word is better than life!

Ponder this. Don't pass over it thinking you know it already. The Word of God is a living thing. When we hold that precious book in our hands, we're holding something that's living and breathing.

For the Word of God is living and powerful, and sharper than any two-edged sword, piercing even to the division of soul and spirit, and of joints and marrow, and is a discerner of the thoughts and intents of the heart. And there is no creature hidden from His sight, but all things are naked and open to the eyes of Him to whom we must give account.

Hebrews 4:12-13

It's living and powerful. It's sharp. It divides, discerns, and has eyes to see. When the Word speaks to us, nothing is hidden from His eyes.

His words are spirit and life.

John 6:63

They are life to all those who find them and health to all their flesh.

Proverbs 4:22

The gospel is the power of God unto salvation.

Romans 1:16

Notice it doesn't say the gospel teaches us about the power, but the gospel *is the power!* The Word of God has resident within itself the power to bring itself to pass. We don't read the Bible just to learn things about God. We read it to know Him! We don't read it just to learn principles and doctrine. We meditate on His Word so He can speak life to us.

Meditating the Word

So, how do we meditate the written Word of God? Biblical meditation is not the same as Eastern meditation, which has its roots in Buddhism and is done through completely emptying the mind. If a person does that, their mind is supposed to become a blank slate so the universe can write upon it whatever it wishes. I cannot express to you how dangerous this is. If your mind becomes a blank slate, the devil will be more than happy to write on it!

Biblical meditation is exactly the opposite of Eastern Meditation. It's not emptying our minds; it's filling them with thoughts of God and His will for our lives from the Scriptures. Here are some simple steps to help you do this:

1. **Meditation should be done in an atmosphere of worship.** This is God we're dealing with. We don't just rush in, open our Bibles, and start reading and meditating. There needs to be a deep reverence for God that fills our hearts. As we worship Him, our hearts are cleansed and our minds are stilled from all other things that compete for our attention.

2. **Ask for the Holy Spirit's help.** We don't need our own wisdom; we need His wisdom. Remember, He wrote the book so only He can reveal it. Remain sensitive to the Holy Spirit as you meditate on the Word.

3. **Personalize the passage.** Turn scriptures into first-person prayers back to God. Personalize a scripture by putting it in the first person, using I, me, and my. Let's use Philippians 4:4-7 as an example:

> Rejoice in the Lord always. Again I will say, rejoice! Let your gentleness be known to all men. The Lord is at hand. Be anxious for nothing, but in everything by prayer and supplication, with thanksgiving, let your requests be made known to God; and the peace of God, which surpasses all understanding, will guard your hearts and minds through Christ Jesus.

My prayer would go something like this: "Lord, I thank You and rejoice in You in all things. Let my gentleness be known to everyone. I'll live my life knowing that Your coming is at hand. I will not be anxious for anything. Instead, by prayer and supplication, with thanksgiving, I will make all my requests and lay all my cares before You. I'm confident that the peace of God, which surpasses all my understanding, will guard my heart and mind through Jesus Christ. Lord, help me to live in the reality of these truths every day."

When we put scripture in the first person, it becomes a living expression within our heart, which is one aspect of meditation.

4. **Give attention to each word of the verse.** Focusing on one verse at a time, quote it to the Lord, pondering each word. With each recitation of a verse, emphasize a different word. For example, if you are meditating on Philippians 4:19, you would emphasize a different word each time you repeated the passage:

> And *MY* God shall supply all my need according to His riches in glory by Christ Jesus.

> And my *GOD* shall supply all my need according to His riches in glory by Christ Jesus.

And my God *SHALL* supply all my need according to His riches in glory by Christ Jesus.

And my God shall *SUPPLY* all my need according to His riches in glory by Christ Jesus.

And my God shall supply *ALL* my need according to His riches in glory by Christ Jesus.

And my God shall supply all *MY* need according to His riches in glory by Christ Jesus.

And my God shall supply all my *NEED* according to His riches in glory by Christ Jesus.

You may have read through those quickly with the emphasis on the highlighted word, but when you're doing this on your own, it takes a bit of time and concentration. Be attentive and speak the words out loud as you continue thinking about the ramifications of each word. This simple method of meditation will reveal new insights and give you greater understanding of phrases and sentences. As you hear the words of the passage, you'll discern nuances and associations often overlooked when the passage is read silently.

5. **Respond to God as He teaches you.** Every passage is to be believed, received, or obeyed. Every insight is to be believed unconditionally. Every promise is to be received by faith. Every command is to be obeyed immediately. You're meditating on God's Word, not just to learn truths, but to apply them to your life. You will not hear God's voice if you are not ready to do what He tells you to do.

> But be doers of the word, and not hearers only, deceiving yourselves. For if anyone is a hearer of the word and not a doer, he is like a man observing his natural face in a mirror; for he observes himself, goes away, and immediately forgets what kind of man he was. But he who looks into the perfect law of liberty and continues in it, and is not a forgetful hearer

but a doer of the work, this one will be blessed in what he does.

James 1:22-25

Many times revelation doesn't come until you put into action what you've heard. Your Bible must be your most treasured possession. The word *Bible* simply means "The Book!" There is no other one like it. This Book is divinely inspired, accurate in the minutest detail, and infused with the very life of God. When you understand the true nature of the Bible, you'll never again treat it casually.

The Bible

Many years ago my dad handed me a book, *God's Plan For Man*, by Finis Jennings Dake. I have received countless blessings from it down through the years. Below is an excerpt concerning the nature and blessing of the written Word. Read it carefully and meditatively. Let it inspire a fresh appreciation for this holy book we call the Bible.

"It is the book that contains the mind of God, the state of man, the way of salvation, the doom of sinners and the happiness of believers. Its doctrines are holy, its precepts binding, its histories true and its decisions immutable. Read it to be wise, believe it to be safe and practice it to be holy. It contains light to direct you, food to support you and comfort to cheer you. It is the traveler's map, the pilgrim's staff, the pilot's compass, the soldier's sword and the Christian's character. Here heaven is opened and the gates of hell disclosed. Christ is its grand subject, our good is its design and the glory of God is its end. It should fill your memory, rule your heart and guide your feet in righteousness and true holiness. Read it slowly, frequently, prayerfully, meditatively, searchingly and devotionally. Study it constantly, perseveringly and industriously. Read it through and through until it becomes part of your being and generates faith that will move mountains.

"It is a mine of wealth, the source of health and a world of pleasure. It is given to you in this life, will be opened at the judgment and will last forever. It involves the highest responsibility, will reward the least to the greatest labor and will condemn all who trifle with its sacred contents. It is a mirror to reflect (James 1:23); a hammer to convict (Jeremiah 23:29); a fire to refine (Jeremiah 23:29); seed to multiply (1 Peter 1:23); water to cleanse (Ephesians 5:26; John 15:3); A lamp to guide (Psalm 119:105); and food to nourish, including milk for babes (1 Peter 2:2); bread for the hungry (Matthew 4:4); meat for men (Hebrews 5:11-14); and honey for dessert (Psalm 19:10); it is rain and snow to refresh (Isaiah 55:10); a sword to cut (Hebrews 4:12); a bow to revenge (Habakkuk 3:9); gold to enrich (Psalm 19:7-10); and power to create life and faith (1 Peter 1:23; Romans 10:17)."

God's Word

My heart hungers and thirsts for God's Word.
Wherever I am and whatever I am doing,
I hear the call above every other sound to come to its pages
and dwell there for a time.

As I plunge into the refreshing coolness of its depths,
I am freed from the dryness
that ever threatens to overtake me as I linger too long
in the affairs of everyday life.

This Word of God is so clear, there can be no misunderstanding
of its meaning.

Within these pages, my thirsting soul is satisfied,
my hungry heart is filled,
my intellect is stirred, and my emotions are brought to peace.

Lord, Your Word gives me strength, courage, and enthusiasm
to live every day to the fullest.

All of the potential I was born with is fulfilled, as Your Word
becomes part of my character and personality.

Your ways are made plain to me as I meditate upon Your precepts.

Through thoughtful study, I am gaining an accurate perception
of Your thoughts concerning me.

Page by page, Your loving countenance is painted
on the canvas of my heart
and Your voice has become dearly familiar to me.

I know You, I love You fervently,
and thank You for Your Word that has
Brought me to You and is transforming me into Your image.

Donna Shelton   5/25/86

---Secret Eleven---

Obedience

The subtitle of this book is *How to Turn Talking with God into Walking with God*. This came from years of puzzling over the scripture found in 1 Thessalonians 5:17 that says to "pray without ceasing." I wanted to be a person of prayer but thought praying without ceasing was an impossible task. Let's be real. We have to go to work or school, spend time with friends and family, mow the lawn, and the list could go on and on. If we view prayer in the traditional sense, it's impossible to pray all the time. As I grew in my relationship with God, I came to realize that prayer was not only talking to God in the morning but also acknowledging Him in everything I did throughout the day.

We're mistaken when we view prayer only as an event where we read our Bibles and talk to God. Prayer must become our *lifestyle*. It's who we are and how we lead our lives. God made us for Himself. Our whole lives belong to Him, not just thirty minutes in the morning before we start our day. Many treat prayer as if we were just checking in with God in the morning and then on the way out, saying, "It was great seeing You. I'll check back in with You tomorrow morning."

Our whole lives are to be spent with and lived for God. Yet, in our present culture Christians are adopting a godless philosophy that has become a fundamental part of their worldview. This affects how we view God and what He expects from us. In this philosophy and worldview we are taught there's to be a separation of faith of the heart and reason of the mind. It is this very philosophy that has led to the misinterpretation of the first amendment to the U.S. Constitution as a separation of church and state. It is very destructive to a life of prayer and obedience that I must give it attention and explain.

An underlying basis for the way we think today and our present worldview stems in a great part from a 19th century philosopher, Soren Kierkegaard. He came to the conclusion that faith and reason were to be used in two different realms. Faith was for God and spiritual things, and reason was for everything else. In his view, it was by faith alone, apart from reason, that we know God. And by reason (the reasoning of our minds), we know everything else. He said faith has its realm, and reason has its realm. He maintained that reason should not intrude upon faith's territory, and faith should not intrude upon reason's territory.

It's interesting that the main place in scripture he used to make his point was the story of Abraham offering Isaac on the altar at God's command. He said Abraham did this with blind faith. In other words, he was saying that Abraham had no reason whatsoever to do this. So, in his view, Abraham was acting in faith's realm where reason had no place. I so wish Kierkegaard would have studied the life of Abraham more thoroughly.

Abraham had many reasons to believe God would raise his son from the dead. First of all, God appeared to him at Moreh. Then He visited him with a supernatural vision. God enabled Abraham to destroy the armies of five kings at one time with three hundred and eighteen servants to deliver his nephew, Lot. God caused Abraham and his wife to supernaturally bear this son, Isaac, when he was one hundred years old. God promised Abraham this would happen, and it did just like He said it would. As you can see, Abraham had many reasons to believe God.

Kierkegaard's philosophy has had two debilitating effects. First, it led Christians to stop thinking! Many say they believe in God and His Word, but they can't effectively defend their faith when it is challenged by the world. For instance, when your child asks why you believe the things you do about God and His Word, the worst thing you can say is, "Just because we believe it," or "That's what the church says." When my sons were growing up, I always told them not to ever be afraid to scrutinize our faith in the Bible. It will never disappoint us. It will always stand the test of reason. In fact, living a life of faith in God is the most reasonable way to live.

Secondly, Kierkegaard's philosophy led to secularism. This is the idea that the spiritual world only includes things like church, belief in God, and prayer. Everything else is secular, meaning our faith has nothing to do with it. Therefore, we're told to keep our faith to ourselves. We're told to do whatever we want to inside the four walls of our church, but don't bring it into the public square. You can readily see how prevalent this is today and now you know why. This is not a biblical worldview.

The Bible teaches us that we live in a spiritual world. God, who is Spirit, created all things; therefore all things are spiritual in cause and nature. There's, no such thing as secular, including our job, our family, government, school, or anything else. Since God is the source or cause of all things, He is also the remedy for all things.

Knowing all of this has significant ramifications when it comes to walking with God and our life of prayer. When we view prayer only as the specific time we spend reading our Bible and talking to God, we have bought into secularism. I reiterate again, prayer is a *lifestyle*. Our whole life is spiritual, and God wants us to involve Him in every part of it. The only way this can be done is through a life of obedience to Him and acknowledging Him in everything. This is the meaning of praying without ceasing.

I want to take great care in explaining this life of obedience, because when we understand its true nature, obeying becomes a blessed joy instead of drudgery. Before delving into obedience, I have to show what a blessing there is for those who obey.

The Nature of Blessing

The first thing God did after He created Adam and Eve was to bless them (Genesis 1:28). God loves to bless His children. He makes it abundantly clear all throughout the Scriptures that He wants His children to live a blessed life.

It occurred to me one day that God was making a statement about His intention for us when He created a garden for man to live in. He didn't create a wilderness or a barren valley, but a luscious garden. Everything in it was filled with beauty, and every tree bore fruit that was delicious to eat. What a blessed life!

The first two chapters of Genesis is the only place in the Scriptures where we can see what life is like without the curse of sin in the earth. There we see God's original intention for us. There was one tree in the Garden they could not eat from. This was not to punish Adam and Eve but to teach them a life of obedience to God. The tree was actually there for their benefit. God knew that the key to enjoying everything else in life was to walk in communion with and obedience to Him.

Some will use the wanderings of Israel in the wilderness as a pattern for Christian living. It goes something like this: Life is full of trials and suffering, but in heaven there will be blessings. Certainly, there were many trials and difficulties during the journey through the wilderness to the Promised Land, but it was only an eleven-day walk! It was their *disobedience* that turned this eleven-day walk into forty years of suffering. God's intention for them was not the wilderness, but the Promised Land.

Life can be full of pain and difficulty, but we're to have a Promised Land mentality—not a wilderness mentality. Those who understand the secret of obedience will find peace in the midst of the storm, strength in adversity, and joy in the time of suffering. Those who walk in disobedience to God turn a season of difficulty into a life of suffering!

If God wants us to live a blessed life, what does that look like? Today, there's a lot of talk about blessing that focuses on "getting things." Yes, God will provide for all our needs, and I believe He will do so abundantly. But when we focus on natural so-called "blessings," we miss the whole point. This mentality produces nothing but worldly, carnal Christians, and I believe it is offensive to God. We can have all the wealth and stuff in the world and still not be blessed.

We must understand the true nature of blessing. If we don't, it will keep us from entering the secret place with the proper attitude. The word *blessing* in the Bible is always spoken of in the singular—not plural. Proverbs 10:22 says, *"The blessing of the Lord makes one rich, and He adds no sorrow with it."* He didn't say the blessing(s) of the Lord makes one rich, but the blessing of the Lord.

Blessing is God's life apparent and obvious in us. It's not at all about God giving us stuff as many think, but about God giving us *Himself.* He is the blessing. Can you understand how seeing the blessing of the Lord as stuff can be offensive to Him? The blessing of this life is secured in prayer and obedience to God in our daily lives.

I am the vine, you are the branches. He who abides in Me, and I in him, bears much fruit; for without Me you can do nothing.

John 15:5

The Bible teaches us that Jesus is the vine and we are the branches. As we stay connected to Jesus, the life flows out of the vine into our lives. This life produces everything else we need. It's all about a relationship—not a formula. Note that *blessing* here is not a verb: it's a noun. It's not an action; it's a condition of life. Those who walk in obedience to God live under an umbrella of His blessing.

Some of the Old Testament names that are ascribed to God reveal a great deal about this blessing. *El Shaddai* means *the All-Sufficient One.* He doesn't just give us everything we need to be sufficient; He is our Sufficiency. *Jehovah Shalom* means *He is our Peace.* He doesn't give peace; He is our peace. *Jehovah Rapha* means *He is our Healer.* He doesn't just heal us; He is our healing. *He is everything we need!*

We come to the prayer room to find Him. This is a great secret, yet so many miss it. Many come to the secret place to get something from

God. They're in need financially, so they ask God to bless them with provision. Then if God doesn't come through for them, they're disappointed. Yet they're missing the whole point. He will provide for us, but He desires us to seek Him as our provision. Many times we don't even know what we need, but He does!

> **And even when you ask, you don't get it because your motives are all wrong—you want only what will give you pleasure.**
>
> **James 4:3, NLT**

When we rush into God's presence with a list of things we want Him to do for us, we often don't realize our motives are wrong. We simply have needs, and we know God tells us to "ask and we shall receive." Yet asking—without seeking to understand God's heart and what He wants for us—causes us to ask for the wrong things or for the right things with the wrong motives. Why does it matter?

When we ask without first discovering what His will is for us, we end up with many unanswered prayers. Then we're disappointed because we think prayer doesn't work. God is not a vending machine where we make a few requests and He dispenses with all kinds of goodies. Prayer is an exploration into the heart of God. He is the treasure hidden in the field of prayer. When we find Him as our blessing, we find everything we need! On the other hand, we think if we get the things we're asking for we'll be happy. But God Himself is the only One who can give us real happiness. He alone knows what we need and what will bring true happiness to our lives.

We need to understand how weak we are when it comes to prayer. We need help. We don't even know how to pray unless the Spirit helps us. We must approach prayer humbly, realizing it is a mystical encounter with the Creator of the Universe. How do we even know how to navigate this relationship between the infinite God and finite man? Thank God, the Spirit helps us!

> **Likewise the Spirit also helps in our weaknesses. For we do not know what we should pray for as we ought, but the Spirit Himself makes intercession for us with groanings which**

cannot be uttered. Now He who searches the hearts knows what the mind of the Spirit is, because He makes intercession for the saints according to the will of God.

Romans 8:26-27

He who knows the mind of God makes intercession for us according to the will of God. The man who thinks he doesn't need the work of the Holy Spirit in his life will never be a praying man. It's the Spirit who draws us into the prayer room. It's the Spirit who gives us direction on how to pray. It's the Spirit who makes the Father known to us.

Ponder this. The moment we humbly enter the secret place, acknowledging our weakness and our need for the Spirit to help us, He goes before the Father and begins praying for us. Then He gets the mind and will of the Father and starts praying through us back to the Father. You will never know the full joy and power in prayer until you experience the Holy Spirit lifting your praying to a higher level than you could do on your own. Only Spirit-enabled praying can help you find the One who is the blessing.

Many times, if we got what we asked for, it would lead us in a wrong direction or be harmful to us. Everything we need is contained in the blessing of the Lord. When we seek His blessing, He adds no sorrow with it. The blessing is in Him.

We can't see the wind, yet we know it's there by what it does. In other words, we see the effect of the wind. We see the trees moving, but we don't actually see the wind that's causing them to move. The blessing of the Lord is the same way. We can't see it, but we know it's there by what it accomplishes in and through us.

He who dwells in the secret place of the Most High Shall abide under the shadow of the Almighty. I will say of the Lord, "He is my refuge and my fortress; My God, in Him I will trust." Surely He shall deliver you from the snare of the fowler And from the perilous pestilence. He shall cover you with His feathers, And under His wings you shall take refuge; His truth shall be your shield and buckler. You shall not be afraid of the terror by night, Nor of the arrow that flies by day, Nor of the pestilence that walks in darkness, Nor of the destruction that lays waste at noonday. A thousand may fall at your side, And ten thousand at your right hand; But it shall not come near you. Only with your eyes shall you look, And see the reward of the wicked. Because you have made the Lord, who is my refuge, Even the Most High, your dwelling place, No evil shall befall you, Nor shall any plague come near your dwelling; For He shall give His angels charge over you, To keep you in all your ways. In their hands they shall bear you up, Lest you dash your foot against a stone. You shall tread upon the lion and the cobra, The young lion and the serpent you shall trample underfoot. "Because he has set his love upon Me, therefore I will deliver him; I will set him on high, because he has known My name. He shall call upon Me, and I will answer him; I will be with him in trouble; I will deliver him and honor him. With long life I will satisfy him, And show him My salvation.

Psalm 91

Oh, what a blessed life this blessing brings to us. What abundant provision! There's no want to those who seek Him. What security and comfort! A sense of wellbeing and wholeness fills our being. What protection! The angels of heaven are dispatched to surround us and keep us safe. All fear is gone, for there's no longer anything to fear. We feel so safe in His arms that neither threats from man nor the devil can make us afraid. Thousands of ills and evils may seem to be unleashed in the world, but we're safe and secure under the shadow of the Almighty.

Dear friends, these things belong only to those who dwell in the secret place of the Most High. This is the blessed life. But dwelling in the secret place is not just spending time in prayer in the morning. Remember, to *dwell* means *to settle down, remain, and make your permanent home there.* This can only be done *through obedience to God throughout the day.* As we can see in the Bible, blessing is always promised to those who obey the Lord.

The Life of Obedience

The life of blessing is reserved for the obedient. There's a carelessness and casualness that has crept into the Church today concerning obeying God's commands. Many think it's their option to pick and choose which ones they will strictly adhere to and which ones are not necessary to obey. We're told if we accept Jesus in our lives, He will give us a happy life and make us successful without being given the conditions for that to happen.

> Now it shall come to pass, if you *diligently obey* the voice of the Lord your God, to *observe carefully all* His commandments which I command you today, that the Lord your God will set you high above all nations of the earth. And all these blessings shall come upon you and overtake you, *because you obey* the voice of the Lord your God.
>
> Deuteronomy 28:1-2

The fact has already been established that God wants to bless us, but He has obligated Himself to do so only *if* we obey Him. Today we emphasize the promises without the commands, but the two go hand-in-hand. People who claim the promises of the Bible without giving careful attention to what commands are attached to them lack understanding of God's plan for their lives. The promises— without His plan—will make us miserable. God's not just interested in making things happen for us. He wants us each to become someone He can use to do mighty things in the earth.

As mentioned earlier, sometimes we don't understand the nature of His commandments. When God said, "You shall not lie," it's not because He's trying to be hard or restrictive. He knows how He designed us. He knows when we lie it destroys our integrity, brings discord in our soul, and causes us to lose self-respect. The Ten Commandments, therefore, are really ten freedoms. When we live by these commandments, we really begin to live a life of freedom! As talking to God changes to walking with God, obedience to Him will change.

These scriptures will become a natural part of who you are, not just something you're supposed to do.

> **And whatever you do in word or deed, do all in the name of the Lord Jesus, giving thanks to God the Father through Him.**
>
> Colossians 3:17

> **Whatever you do, do it heartily, as to the Lord and not to men.**
>
> Colossians 3:23

Before I grasped this concept, I would come out of my time of prayer in the morning with a sense of God's grace on my life. But then I would go about my daily activities, not thinking much about Him the rest of the day. By the end of the day, I would wonder why all that grace leaked out of me!

If every activity we engage in is done while acknowledging God, thanking Him and listening for Him to speak to us, our lives will become a continual prayer unto the Lord. This is not hard to do. In fact, it's much easier than you might think. When we spend all our time never acknowledging the Holy Spirit or being sensitive to Him, we'll find it much more difficult to switch gears and let Him take the lead. Our minds are leading the way. This is what it means to be carnally minded or ruled by the mind (Romans 8:5-6). This kind of living leads to spiritual death.

When our mind is in control instead of the Spirit, it drains the grace that fills our spiritual life out of us. We end up spiritually cold and dry. After a few days of this, we find it difficult to sense God's presence when we pray. We must never forget that the phrase "pray without ceasing" is living in communion with God throughout the day.

> **Blessed is the man who walks not in the counsel of the ungodly, nor stands in the path of sinners, nor sits in the seat of the scornful; but his delight is in the law of the Lord, and in His law he meditates *day and night*. He shall be like a tree**

planted by the rivers of water, that brings forth its fruit in its season, whose leaf also shall not wither; and whatever he does shall prosper.

Psalm 1:1-3

There are several important keys to walking with God that are found in these verses. First of all, the person who lives in union with God walks in the counsel of God. We're constantly inundated with voices vying for our attention. There are way too many opinions out there on how we should conduct business, deal with our finances, make decisions, raise our kids, and in general, how we should run our lives! These are the voices of natural, human wisdom. Some of them may be right, while others may be wrong. Whether they're right or wrong, they're limited by the natural mind.

Only God has all the information needed to guide our lives correctly. He has the master plan for our lives, and He desires for us to seek His wisdom so He can give it to us. When we seek His counsel, we're honoring the One who created us. Asking God for direction throughout the day keeps us united to Him. As we involve Him in the details of our lives, this is a form of prayer. When we go throughout the day, never asking what He thinks or wants, we're excluding God from the affairs of our lives.

Many think because they prayed in the morning, God should bless them throughout the day. It doesn't work that way. God comes where He's invited. When we have a decision to make but don't seek His counsel, we become a little more distant from Him. Asking God's opinion brings Him near. Even when God has nothing to say on the matter, the closeness that comes when we acknowledge Him is the reward in itself. Many troubles and heartache could be avoided if we would simply ask, "God, what is Your opinion on this matter?" If we do this throughout the day, we'll be surprised at how near the presence of the Holy One remains.

Secondly, sin separates us from God (Isaiah 59:2). When we live carelessly, yielding to things we know displease God, we may think it really doesn't matter that much. We may think, *It was only a small sin, right?* But even a bad attitude or acting selfishly can separate us from God. Many wonder why God doesn't stay near them throughout the day, yet they take no thought that He is a Holy God and will never be united with unholiness.

Being careless and walking in sin at any time throughout the day greatly affects our time in prayer. It's why we suddenly feel distant from God when we come before Him in prayer. If we have not stayed close to Him throughout the day, we cannot expect to have sweet fellowship with Him. Again, this is a love relationship. Really, it's not about the sin; it's about a broken relationship. God is not withholding His presence because He's mad at us, but because our sin separates us from Him. This hurts His heart. Remember, God is in love with us!

When you're tempted to sin, think of what it will cost you in the loss of God's presence. It will be a great deterrent to yielding to that sin. Why don't you put it to the test? Every time a temptation of any kind comes your way, stop and say, *"Oh, God, I don't want anything to come between You and me. Help me in this moment to say 'No!' to this sin."* Then thank Him and give Him the glory for your victory. Watch what happens the next time you close the door and enter the secret place! The reward will be sweetness to your soul. This also is praying without ceasing.

Thirdly, God is love (1 John 4:8). Abiding in love throughout the day will keep the presence of the Holy Spirit near. We have many opportunities to get in strife with others, to be hurt, and to hold grudges. *We must be relentless about walking in love!* When we hold unforgiveness against someone, we're not hurting him or her. We're hurting ourselves. Someone once said unforgiveness is like drinking poison and hoping the other person will die.

More importantly, when we don't love our neighbor unconditionally, God becomes distant. Jesus said we are to love our enemies. We cannot say we're unable to love someone because of what he or she did to us. This isn't about the person or what he or she did! It's about staying close to Jesus. We must purposefully love difficult people. The reward will be great in the secret place.

The Psalmist said blessed is the person who does these things. The blessing of God upon your life is at stake. Go back and meditate on Psalm 91. This blessing is worth whatever price you have to pay!

Repentance

I'm so grateful God has offered us the grace of repentance! The Bible tells us that King David was a man who committed many gross sins, but he also was a man who was quick to repent. None of us are going to live without sin, so we must be quick to repent. If we fall into sin throughout the day, we must quickly come to our heavenly Father with deep sorrow for our sin and ask Him to forgive us. Then when we return to the prayer room, God has forgotten our sin and His presence will be sweet.

> If we say that we have no sin, we deceive ourselves, and the truth is not in us. If we confess our sins, He is faithful and just to forgive us our sins and to cleanse us from all unrighteousness.
>
> 1 John 1:8-9

Brother Lawrence, who wrote the book, *The Practice of the Presence of God*, lived in the 1600s. Let's take a look at some of the quotes from his book and learn from them:

> "A thought of Him from time to time, a little act of adoration, sometimes to ask for His grace, sometimes to offer Him your sufferings, at other times to thank Him for the graces, past and present, He has bestowed on you, in the midst of your troubles to take solace in Him as often as you can. Lift up your heart to Him during your meals and in company; the least little remembrance will always be the most pleasing to Him. One need not cry out very loudly; He is nearer to us than we think."

In essence, this is how we pray without ceasing. We view many of the things we do as distractions from "spiritual" things. We work away at our jobs doing things we think has nothing to do with God. We may even think, *How can God get any glory out of this?* Yet this was one of Brother Lawrence's best secrets to practicing God's presence, and we can practice it also with some thought and diligence. If, from time to time, we were to lift our thoughts toward God and thank Him for the strength and wisdom to do this work, God would be glorified, and we would be drawn near to Him once again through it. These moments would become acts of prayer.

When someone mistreats us in some way, we could offer a quick prayer of thankfulness for His love for us. He never rejects or finds fault with us as humans do. If we're in a place where it's not possible to pray out loud, then just the lifting of our thoughts to Him would accomplish the same thing. In the midst of suffering, a brief prayer of trust in God would bring us back into the presence of God and bring glory to Him. When something good happens throughout the day, we could breathe a quick prayer of thanks and go on with our day. *The length of the prayer does not determine its effectiveness, but rather the heart from which it's prayed!*

Brother Lawrence also wrote, "*We ought not to be weary of doing little things for the love of God, who regards not the greatness of the work, but the love with which it is performed.*"

Often we think of thanking God for the big things, but I believe God is most pleased when we think of Him in the little things. God wants to be involved in the smallest things in our lives, and when we think of Him in these moments, it tells God that's what we want, too.

At one point, Brother Lawrence was given the job of washing the dishes for everyone in the monastery. He hated this job. He said all he wanted to do was to spend time with God in prayer. God told Him if he would thank Him every time he washed a dish and did it as unto the Lord, He would receive it as an act of prayer. When he began to do this, all heaven opened up, and God's presence filled the room.

Brother Lawrence wrote:

Our sanctification did not depend upon changing our works, but in doing that for GOD'S sake, which we commonly do

for our own. That it was lamentable to see how many people mistook the means for the end, addicting themselves to certain works, which they performed very imperfectly, by reason of their human or selfish regards.

We mistakenly think things like prayer, reading the Bible, going to church, and being involved in ministry activities are the only spiritual things in our lives. Many Christians wish they could be in full-time ministry so they can give themselves more fully to God. But it's not the type of work we do that makes it holy; it's what we do for the sake of God and to honor Him that makes it holy. As Christians we need to stop saying we work in a godless place, but instead, bring God to the work place by doing all we do as unto the Lord.

In my early years of ministry, I spent all day Saturday in prayer preparing to minister on Sunday. My wife was given instructions to not let the boys come into my study regardless of the situation. I would rise very early Sunday morning to pray until it was time to go to church. I would also drive a separate car to church from my wife and kids, so I wouldn't be interrupted while I prayed in the car. I thought this was very spiritual.

One Sunday, my two youngest boys, ages four and six, asked if they could ride to church with me. I said, "Absolutely not!" I was not about to let them rob me of my last few minutes with God before I preached. But they kept begging me until I finally relented. I proceeded to tell them if they were going with me, they needed to leave right then because I was ready to leave.

Their hair was standing straight up so I had to go back into the house and comb it. This frustrated me. Then I saw they didn't have their shoes on, so we set out to find their shoes. One of their shoes was nowhere to be found. After looking for several minutes, I found the shoe in the trunk of my car! I have no idea how it ended up there. I put their shoes on, put them in the back seat of the car, and said, "Don't say a word. Daddy is going to be praying!"

When we passed by a McDonald's restaurant, my boys said, "Daddy can we stop at McDonald's? We haven't had anything to eat."

Reluctantly, I pulled into McDonald's and ordered two biscuits. As we were pulling out, one of the boys said, "Daddy, Daddy, they didn't give us any jelly." I was very upset by this time. My boys had totally taken me out of my deeply "spiritual" time with God. I pulled back into McDonald's and curtly said, "Give me two jellies!"

By the time I headed for church, I had such a bad attitude I could no longer pray. When I arrived, I went into a room, sat down, and said, "God, I'm sorry for letting these boys steal my anointing. If you'll just anoint me to preach this one time, I promise I'll never let these boys ride with me to church again!"

Then God said something that totally shocked me. He asked, "Rick, do you have sons?"

I thought this was an odd question since my sons had just caused me all this trouble.

"Yes, Lord," I said. "You know I do."

"That means you're a father, right?" He said and proceeded to ask, "Do you have a wife? Do you have parents? Do you have friends?"

"Of course, Lord," I said.

"That means you're a husband, a son, and a friend, right?" He asked.

"Lord, what are You getting at?" I responded.

He said, "All of these are roles I've called you to, and whatever I've called you to do, I've anointed you to do it. You think the only time you're spiritual and anointed is when you're praying, reading your Bible, or preaching. If you will understand that you're called and anointed to do all these other things in your life, you will walk in My presence doing these things as much as you do in the things you deem to be spiritual activity."

This stunned me! I repented on the spot. From that time on, I spent time with my kids on Saturday, instead of praying all day. The difference was I began to do these things as unto the Lord, and the grace of God was greatly evidenced on my life. I began to understand that day that my entire life is an act of prayer when I do it for the glory of God. This set me free from a pharisaical spirit. This is also what it means to "pray without ceasing."

The Lord's Love Language

Here I am, Lord, and I have come gratefully offering my gifts of love.

I speak the language MY heart understands, but I want you
to take me into Your chamber and help me comprehend the words
that touch *You* to the very core.

What is Your love language? What do You long to hear coming
from my heart to Yours?

I've been reading over and over Bro. Lawrence's book about
practicing Your presence and that is what I am trying to do.

I would venture to suppose from all my reading in the Bible and
about great men and women of God that three things are at least a
part of Your love language and the secret to Your Abiding Presence.

The first would be, simply loving You for who you are. Period.

A close second to that would be obeying You
because we love you so much.

Then out of us would spring continual thanksgiving for Your sweet,
abiding presence that comes from doing the first two.

Just pondering that today. Guess You will let me know if I was right
when I see You, but it is my joy to do them regardless.

I'm so filled up with love for You.

Donna Shelton
2005

---Secret Twelve---

Repentance

Some words in the Bible are viewed only negatively, and *repentance* is certainly one of those words. This is mostly due to a lack of understanding, as many people think of repentance as groveling in shame and condemnation before an angry God. This could not be further from the truth. Repentance is a beautiful gift given to us by our loving Father to help us get back on our feet and begin running with Him again. This gift is not meant to punish but to restore us.

Think of it this way: If God had not given us this gift of repentance, we would be left hopelessly in our sins. Repentance is a pathway into the secret place. When God visited Moses in the burning bush, He said, "Do not draw near this place. Take your sandals off your feet, for the place where you stand is holy ground" (Exodus 3:5). Taking shoes off is a symbol of repentance. It's saying, "God, where I've been in my walk and what I've done is not worthy of You. I'm sorry for the dirt that is on these shoes. I repent, Lord, for what I have done." God wasn't mad at Moses or trying to push him away. He was inviting him into His presence, but he could not come with his shoes on.

We must understand this about repentance. When God gives us the opportunity to repent, it's not so He can punish us. Instead, He's extending His grace to us. It's the means to restore us to a place of innocence and purity. Repentance is simply accepting the guilt of our wrong, asking forgiveness for the sin, and deciding to turn away from it to follow Jesus once again.

> **Therefore, having these promises, beloved, let us cleanse ourselves from all filthiness of the flesh and spirit, perfecting holiness in the fear of God. For even if I made you sorry with my letter, I do not regret it; though I did regret it. For I perceive that the same epistle made you sorry, though only for a while. Now I rejoice, not that you were made sorry, but that your sorrow led to repentance. For you were made sorry in a godly manner, that you might suffer loss from us in nothing. For godly sorrow produces repentance leading to salvation, not to be regretted; but the sorrow of the world produces death. For observe this very thing, that you sorrowed in a godly manner: What diligence it produced in you, what clearing of yourselves, what indignation, what fear, what vehement desire, what zeal, what vindication! In all things you proved yourselves to be clear in this matter.**
>
> **2 Corinthians 7:1, 8-11**

The first thing we need to know about repentance is that it comes from conviction, not condemnation. There's a vast difference between the two! Satan is constantly accusing us to bring condemnation. Condemnation is the expression of very strong disapproval and the action of condemning someone to a punishment. When we experience condemnation, we feel God is mad at us. We have a sense that we need to be punished for what we have done. There's heaviness and no hope for us in this condition.

Conviction on the other hand comes from the Holy Spirit. Conviction is a formal declaration that someone is guilty of a criminal offense, made by the verdict of a jury or the decision of a judge in a court of law. Both condemnation and conviction judge us of wrong, but condemnation judges us wrongly. Conviction is the Holy Spirit placing a judgment against our sin rightly according to the Law of God. Verse ten of the passage above reads, *"Godly sorrow produces repentance leading to salvation, not to be regretted; but the sorrow of the world produces death."*

When Satan condemns us, we feel sentenced to death. This is what Paul called worldly sorrow. There seems to be no way out. We feel hopeless. This is actually designed to make us feel so unworthy we think God doesn't want to see our faces. Many people have wrongly felt there was no other option but to take their own lives, so great was the guilt and condemnation for the wrong they had done. If only they knew or remembered that Jesus came and gave His life because there was no other way to be rid of that guilt except through Him.

Again, when the Holy Spirit convicts us, it's not to punish us but to restore us and lead us back to salvation. This is godly sorrow. Yes, we need to feel the full weight of our sin, own up to it, and feel deeply sorry for it. But this is only designed to get us back on track with God and to fall madly in love with Jesus again! If God didn't convict us, but left us to go on in our sin, He wouldn't be a loving Father at all.

Don't miss this next point. When we feel condemned, usually we're sorry because we got caught for something or because of the negative consequences our sin caused others and us. On the other hand, when we're convicted, we're sorry because we offended our Father and caused a separation in our relationship with Him. We should never view sin in isolation as just something we have done wrong. We must look at sin in view of how it affected our relationship with God. In the mind of God, the broken relationship is always the issue, not the sin itself.

There's really only one sin, and that's the sin of rejecting Christ. The Holy Spirit convicts us of this sin because we've not trusted in Christ to give us everything we need to make us satisfied and fulfilled (John 16:8-9). All sin is a temptation to find gratification in things other than what can only be found in Him. Sin entices us with the promise that it will thrill us and make us happy, but it always leaves us empty and feeling condemned.

David's Prayer of Repentance

The beautiful prayer King David wrote in Psalm 51 shows his repentant heart, a heart God said was after His own.

> For I acknowledge my transgressions, And my sin is always before me. Against You, You only, have I sinned, And done this evil in Your sight—That You may be found just when You speak, And blameless when You judge.

> **Psalm 51:3-4**

David had committed adultery with Bathsheba and had her husband murdered! His sin was against others, but he said, "Against You, You only have I sinned." David spent all his years growing up alone with God. He knew what it was like to live in the presence of God in a beautiful, close, loving relationship with Him. The thing that broke his heart and made him feel sorrow was the broken relationship with God that his sin caused. It wasn't enough to feel it, David had to repent and ask God to do what only He could do.

> Create in me a clean heart, O God, And renew a steadfast spirit within me. Do not cast me away from Your presence, And do not take Your Holy Spirit from me.

> **Psalm 51:10-11**

David realized he had sinned terribly, so he prayed that God would wash him of his corruption, cleanse him of the filth of his sin, and give him back what he so treasured—a clean heart. Then came this cry from the depths of his soul: "*Oh, God, please, do not cast me away from Your presence, and whatever You do, do not take Your Holy Spirit from me!*" Can you hear the desperate plea born out of what he realized was most precious to him in life?

Oh, dear Christian, realize that momentary pleasures of sin are robbing us of that which we long for the most! When we live with unclean hearts, God is not angry with us. His heart is broken over our sin because it separates us from Him. Remember, above all else, God is a Father. He is *your* Father. He always wants the best for you and longs to hold you close in His arms.

One time when I was a teenager, my friend and I stayed out all night. I told my parents I was staying at his house, and he told his parents he was staying at my house. Oh, what fun we had that night! At dawn, when I returned home, I quietly turned the knob to the front door, but suddenly it was opened from the inside. There in front of me stood my dad. I cannot describe to you what terror flowed through me. I realized I had been caught in my sin.

When I looked into my father's eyes, what I saw surprised me. I didn't see anger. Of course, he was very unhappy with me but what happened next impacted me forever. The only words my dad said were, *"Son, why did you do this? Why did you lie to us? I'm disappointed in you."* Those words broke my heart. Any punishment would have hurt much less than this did.

That experience changed me. I realized my dad loved me so much that he placed restrictions on what I could, and couldn't do, for my benefit. The things I thought were restraints were there to protect me.

In Matthew 7:11, Jesus tells us that as good as our earthly parents can be, our heavenly Father is so much better:

If you then, being evil, know how to give good gifts to your children, how much more will your Father who is in heaven give good things to those who ask Him!

If you've fallen into things that displease the Lord or have grown distant from Him, look into His loving eyes and hear Him say, *"My child, why did you do this? Don't you know I have told you the things you should and shouldn't do are not to be hard on you, but to protect you because I love you? I want the very best for you."*

The Fruit of Repentance

Many people see the only benefit of repentance as being a restored relationship with God, but there's so much more. Let's take a surprising journey into the world of repentance. Continuing on with 2

Corinthians 7, Paul builds on what he had been saying to the Corinthian believers about his convicting letter. *"What diligence it produced in you, what clearing of yourselves, what indignation, what fear, what vehement desire, what zeal, what vindication! In all things you proved yourselves to be clear in this matter"(verse 7).*

1. "What Diligence it Produced in You"

When we fall into sin, walls of righteousness that were built up in our lives to protect us from temptation and sin have been torn down. We cross lines and open ourselves to wrong influences that are hard to erase. When the Holy Spirit convicts us of these things and we truly repent, the protecting walls are restored. The enemy's influence is destroyed over our lives. We now have a renewed diligence to walk in righteousness and resist temptation.

Think of your life as a house you're building for the Holy Spirit to inhabit. Brick by brick, you're becoming stronger in your faith, more pure and holy in your walk, more righteous in your behavior and attitude, and more loving in your relationships. You're doing all this that God may be glorified by this house you're becoming.

Paul called our lives a building that is being built (1 Corinthians 3:9-11). He said be careful how you build it. The foundation of the entire building must be Jesus. Staying close to Him is the key to the building standing strong through the storms of life. These walls are our defenses from attacks and temptations of the enemy. Every time we give place to *any sin*, it tears down another brick in our wall of righteousness. If we continue in sin, eventually the walls of our house are destroyed and a stronghold of unrighteousness takes its place in that area. We then become vulnerable to every temptation.

In the Old Testament, great walls were built around a city as a fortress against the attacks of their enemies. When these walls were broken down, they were not only vulnerable, but were also sure to be attacked. It was an open invitation to an enemy. It was not a matter of potentially being overrun and conquered, it was inevitable they would be. In the same way, every time we yield to a temptation to sin, more of our walls of righteousness are torn down (Proverbs 25:28).

If we continue in sin, we have no defense whatsoever! Yielding to sin destroys our will to resist the enemy. So, Satan and sin come and go as they please. At this point, we may make a decision that we're tired of sin and what it has done to us, but we find we're helpless to do so. We're trapped by what we've given place to in our lives.

In Genesis 4:7, Cain had already given place to the sin of anger and jealousy. God confronted him on it and said, *"If you do well, will you not be accepted? And if you do not do well, sin lies at the door. And its desire is for you, but you should rule over it."* God is telling him that he has to get a hold of himself and stop yielding to these sins. If he doesn't, God lets him know that greater, stronger sins are lurking in the dark, waiting to lure him in to the point where he's fully controlled by sin.

We never intend to fall under the control of sin. We just think we can dabble in it here and there and get away with it. What we don't realize is that this is the way Satan works. He will begin by tempting us with sins like anger and jealousy that seem innocuous. Other sins would be unforgiveness, pride, greed, and selfishness. We may feel these don't present any real danger because they're inside us and many times others don't know we're giving into them. Another great deception is to think these aren't really sin, just bad attitudes. Yet they all come from Satan, and he has a bigger plan. It begins with gradually enticing us to sin in order to eventually gain control over us! The little sins open the door for the bigger ones.

Too many people draw the battle line against sin at the wrong place—the place of their actions. The battle line against sin should be drawn at the place of our thought life! The first place our walls of righteousness are torn down is in our minds. What we allow to control our minds will eventually control our lives!

> **Well then, since God's grace has set us free from the law, does that mean we can go on sinning? Of course not! Don't you realize that you become the slave of whatever you choose to obey? You can be a slave to sin, which leads to death, or you can choose to obey God, which leads to righteous living.**
>
> **Romans 6:15-16, NLT**

As Christians, none of us want to be controlled by sin. Jesus is our Lord, and we desire to be under His authority. What I'm trying to tell you emphatically is that sin is deceitful. It's your enemy, not your friend. Sin lies to you, promising you a happy life then leaves you under its control. You never intend for it to happen, but it becomes your master.

Thank God for repentance! The moment we're honestly sorry for our sin, turn from it, and repent, the slate is wiped clean. We're declared not guilty and by the grace of God the protective walls of righteousness are restored. This isn't the end of it, though. There's still work to be done. Satan will come again to try to drag you back into the same sin. If you'll run to your heavenly Father in the secret place and lay it before Him, He'll give you the grace and strength of His Holy Spirit to conquer the enemy and gain victory over temptation.

Each time you gain a victory, the walls of righteousness will become stronger. Eventually, you will come to the place where that sin won't bother you anymore. What a blessed place this is where Satan has nothing on us, and there's nothing that stands between God and us! The goal is not just to conquer the sin. Our focus must be on keeping ourselves in a place where we can enter in to sweet communion with God without any sense of guilt, shame, or unworthiness. Isn't this the life we all long to have?

2. "What Clearing of Yourselves"

In order to sin, we have to resist the voice of the Holy Spirit inside us. Each time we override His voice of conviction, our conscience becomes weaker and weaker. The longer we sin, the more our conscience is seared. Eventually our hearts become hardened. At this point, we can sin without being bothered by it at all. This is a frightening place to be! When we truly repent and ask God to renew a right spirit within us, our hearts are softened, our conscience is renewed, and once again we become sensitive to the Holy Spirit. We'll feel Him inside, telling us to say no to that temptation, and He'll immediately give us grace and strength to overcome it.

Treasure the voice of the Spirit within you. Learn to obey the slightest promptings. The more you listen and obey, the stronger His voice will become. Hearing the voice of God and being sensitive to the promptings of the Holy Spirit keeps you safe and gives you direction. Remember, you're not talking into the air but to God, and He's listening, always ready to help and deliver you.

The easiest and most sure way to learn to hear God's voice is to let Him speak to you through the Scriptures. Find a passage of scripture, meditate on it, let it speak to you, and then ask the Holy Spirit to make it a part of your life. One word from heaven can bring you far more pleasure than all the world has to offer. Let me encourage you to read Deuteronomy 28:1-14 to see some of the blessings God gives His people.

3. "What Indignation"

The more we give ourselves to sin, the more we fall in love with it. This is the very nature of sin. Sin makes itself very attractive and alluring to the flesh. If I may be blunt, let me show you something about sin. All sin by nature is filthy, dirty, and rotten to the core. But on the surface, it can be very attractive. It looks like just the thing you want or need, but inside it's rotten and will bring that into your spirit as defilement.

For example, let's consider adultery and make it applicable. A man or woman may be attracted to a person at work. At first there is harmless flirting with words of admiration. Their mate seems boring compared to the adventure an affair will give. Before long that person will be allured by the mystery and thrill of stolen fruit. It will seem so right. They will be deluded to feel like soul mates instead of adulterers. In the process, they'll lose their integrity, the marriage will be destroyed, and the kids will be terribly wounded. In the end, they'll realize they were enticed to trade all the good in their lives for the seduction of sin.

One of the gravest enticements to sin is through pornography. It's everywhere and available on every kind of media. What used to be shameful is now blazed openly and made to seem glamorous. There's no industry so descriptive of the outward allure but inward rottenness of sin and defilement as this. It's so sad that many Christians who love God have a stronghold of addiction to pornography. When you make that fateful click on your computer, you're at first appalled, but if you don't immediately and forcefully turn it off, you just can't resist watching. When you're finished, you are left feeling filthy and guilty. You can't believe you did it. Sin is always this way. On the front end, it offers you gratification, but on the back end, it leaves you feeling dirty and disgusted with yourself.

Nothing about sin will bring true happiness. As with all sin, the momentary pleasure will end, and the false beauty will fade into the real ugliness that can't remain hidden. You will be empty, wondering how you could have let yourself buy into the lie.

If you want to come to the place where you hate the sin, you must see it as the filth it really is. The only thing that can produce this hatred for sin is you seeing how offended your heavenly Father is over it. He is broken-hearted that giving into this sin has taken you away from His presence.

Whatever you do, don't try to hide your sin when you pray. This is foolishness. God knows all about it, beginning with the first thoughts of temptation you listened to all the way to the sin at its end. The most beautiful and precious thing about the secret place is that it's a safe place to lay all your sin on the table. You can be real and transparent with God. In fact, that's what pleases Him the most. Never forget King David who God said was a man after His own heart. This seems incredible in the light of all the terrible things he did. Yet it was David's heart, quick to acknowledge and repent of sin, that was so precious and valuable to God.

Tell God everything. Spill out you heart and don't try to be spiritual. When you sin, repent. Tell Him how you gave into temptation, and ask Him to give you strength and grace to be stronger against it. If you have doubts, tell them to Him. If you feel something is not fair, ask Him about it. Don't hide anything from Him. Be real. What you're thinking or feeling may not be right, but God is never offended with honesty. He can straighten you out, and you'll be brought closer to Him in the process.

Again, the secret place is holy. You'll never find it if you bring sin that you've not repented of with you. You may do something you think is prayer, but you'll never enter the secret place of His presence. The beauty of grace is that the moment we confess our sin with true godly sorrow forgiveness is immediately extended to us. Our spirits are cleansed, and we're instantly restored to a loving relationship with God. Oh, what a wonder Savior we serve!

4. "What Fear"

We're admonished to fear God in the Scriptures more than three hundred times. It must not be treated as a side doctrine. Because it was dealt with earlier, suffice it to say that the fear of the Lord is the key to developing a holy hatred of sin and departing from it (Proverbs 8:13; 16:6). Thank God, when we truly repent, the fear of the Lord is restored. We then want to live our lives pleasing to Him because of our high regard for Him and for what He has done for us in giving us His Son. Oh, what a protection this fear is from a careless and unruly life!

5. "What Vehement Desire"

When we sin or disobey God, the most devastating consequence is that it causes a separation from God. Think carefully over what I'm going to say next because this is where many people miss it. Separation from God hasn't come because He has turned His back on us. He's withholding His presence from us because our love for Him has grown cold. If you're experiencing separation from God in your life, it's because sin has become your new lover.

James 4:1-5 lays this out quite clearly:

Where do wars and fights come from among you? Do they not come from your desires for pleasure that war in your members? You lust and do not have. You murder and covet and cannot obtain. You fight and war. Yet you do not have because you do not ask. You ask and do not receive, because

you ask amiss, that you may spend it on your pleasures. Adulterers and adulteresses! Do you not know that friendship with the world is enmity with God? Whoever therefore wants to be a friend of the world makes himself an enemy of God. Or do you think that the Scripture says in vain, "The Spirit who dwells in us yearns jealously"?

This is stunning! Some may be uncomfortable with this raw language, but the Bible is full of it.

God calls His children who have fallen into sin "adulterers and adulteresses." He calls their pursuit for happiness in the things of this world lust. This is the language of a scorned lover. I find it amazing that God, who is self-existent and needs nothing outside Himself, has placed Himself in a position where He yearns jealously for our love.

We know that on our own merit we don't deserve to be in the secret place with God, but we're there because He has invited us. He paid the most expensive price ever paid that we might be able to stand in His presence without any sense of guilt, shame, or unworthiness. Only sin robs us of our desire to be with Him in prayer.

This ought to be our greatest motivation to turn from sin and repent. Just think of how foolish and deceitful sin is. Satan woos us with the temptation of a thrill that will last for only a moment, yet robs us of our desire to be wrapped in unconditional love for eternity. Thank God, once our eyes are opened and we turn from our sin, a vehement, intensely emotional desire returns for the presence of God. When our heart is right, there will be a burning desire to be with God.

Let's be done with this lukewarm, complacent Christianity! If you have little or no desire to be with God in prayer, you're in a dangerous place spiritually. Just as losing our appetite for food is a sign we're sick physically, so losing our appetite for prayer is a sign we're sick spiritually.

Revelation 2:2-5 describes a church that had departed from their love for God. Jesus told John to write to them and say:

"I know your works, your labor, your patience, and that you cannot bear those who are evil. And you have tested those who say they are apostles and are not, and have found them liars; and you have persevered and have patience, and have labored for My name's sake and have not become weary. Nevertheless I have this against you, that *you have left your first love.* Remember therefore from where you have fallen; repent and do the first works, or else I will come to you quickly and remove your lampstand from its place—unless you repent."

You may be a faithful church member and even be involved in ministry, yet you have lost the love for God you had when you first found Christ. If so, you've lost everything! Remember what it was like when you were most in love with Jesus? What were you doing then? Go back and do it again. We can become so preoccupied with the activities of the church we can forget the God for whom these activities exist.

What do we do if we find ourselves in this place, having walked away from our first love? Exactly what Jesus tells this church: Repent! Oh, what joy fills our hearts when, through a simple prayer of repentance, vehement desire for God arises in our souls once again! No one else can take His place. Nothing else will do but to feel the warmth of His embrace. Remember what a priceless treasure He is, and you will gladly lay everything else down to be in His presence.

6. "What Zeal"

Zeal means *a strong feeling of interest and enthusiasm that makes someone very eager or determined to do something.* When you truly repent of sin and are forgiven, a strong feeling of interest and enthusiasm for God and pleasing Him begins to burn inside you again.

When Christians don't pray, they become complacent about the work God has called them to and to their place in the church. Much of modern Christianity has become consumer-oriented. We think the church exists to bless and serve us. We become spectators instead of participators. A casualness and even a lack of respect for the house of God creeps in.

The church is precious to Jesus. It's His bride. When we lack strong interest and enthusiasm for the church, we're disrespecting His bride. A lack of zeal for the house of God is a sure indication that repentance is needed. When we truly repent, a zeal for the house of God returns to us. Nothing will keep us away from church. We want to be there every time the doors are open. We sit on the edge of our seats to hear the Word preached. We worship with abandonment. We become eager volunteers. We have a desire to be discipled and raised up to fulfill what God has called us to do.

7. "What vindication"

To be *vindicated* means *to show that someone should not be blamed for a crime or mistake, to show that someone is not guilty.* We're not guilty! What a wonderful thing it is to hear this pronounced over our lives. We've not only been forgiven, but we've been judged innocent by the supreme judge of the universe. There's no higher court whereby Satan can appeal. He may continue to accuse us, but the verdict has already been rendered. We've been pronounced not guilty, and even better, the entire record of our sin is erased!

> You were dead because of your sins and because your sinful nature was not yet cut away. Then God made you alive with Christ, for He forgave all our sins. He canceled the record of the charges against us and took it away by nailing it to the cross. In this way, He disarmed the spiritual rulers and authorities. He shamed them publicly by His victory over them on the cross.
>
> Colossians 2:13-16

I've heard that many times people who've been in prison for a long time struggle for a while after being released. They're just not used to a life of freedom. Many Christians struggle this way too. But Christ didn't just pardon us; He took our sin upon Himself and pronounced us not guilty. This is the marvelous grace of redemption. He not only forgave us of our sin, but He released us from the responsibility of paying any penalty for it. His substitution gives us the full rights of a citizen who had never committed a crime.

We don't have to look over our shoulder, fearing that our past sin is catching up with us in some way. It 's gone! In fact, Jeremiah said God doesn't even remember our forgiven sin (Jeremiah 31:34). If God doesn't remember our past sins, then why are we still remembering them? When we sin and are forgiven, we're not second-class citizens in the kingdom of God. He doesn't resort to a Plan B for our lives because we've messed up Plan A. Sometimes we may feel we've wasted too much time in sin, but God has a way of redeeming the time. He can speed things up and get us back on course as if no time has been lost.

These thoughts are not intended to treat sin lightly, but to show how powerful and glorious the work of the cross is in our life. These truths affect how we view our standing with God and our access to the secret place of prayer.

Once you've repented of your sin, never bring it up to God again. I could spend the rest of my days in prayer thanking Him and talking to Him about all that Jesus did for me on the cross! I could talk about the unimaginable suffering He endured in my place, His innocent blood shed for my guilty blood. He could have come down from the cross when the pain became intolerable. He could have called ten thousand angels to rescue Him, but He didn't. He stayed there so we could have life. I could go on and on, but you get the point. There's so much fuel for prayer in this one fact. Because of the cross, we've been vindicated.

Temptation

Temptation has stalked you, biding its time
You thought it was gone, it was lagging behind.

Drooling with hunger to snare you once more
Enticing you always to open the door.

With thoughts not controlled, it creeps right on in
Aiming to fester and manifest sin.

Driven by malice, a stronghold to build
Till your heart and thought-life with evil are filled.

Sin wants to have you, and you have a choice
Heaven and hell waits the sound of your voice.

If there is silence, hell knows it has won
It means you are weakening and considering some.

Your flesh will join in and add all of its weight
The scales are now tipped; it is almost too late.

I am imprisoned by your choice and will
My heart weeps within you and draws you until

The scales of deception are taken away
And seeing your sin, you fall down and pray.

Open your eyes now, look in My face
You thought you'd see anger; you will see grace.

I made you, remember, you're My heart's desire
I know all your weakness, and I'll never tire

Of lifting you always whenever you fall
I hear your heart cry, even when you don't call.

Donna Shelton
10/10/1993

Repentance

He placed His finger under my chin, lifting my face,
I couldn't look at Him.

So full of shame I trembled at His touch...my heart was all broken,
I'd hurt Him so much.

I promised the last time I committed this sin;
I'd be strong next time and not do it again.

My pain is now double, I must run away...
I lied and I sinned and have nothing to say.

Caught by His Spirit, convicted, brought near,
my face in His hands—what will I hear.

He knows that I love Him and long to do right,
yet, so weak I fell with hardly a fight.

O Jesus! My Savior! I'm sorry! I cry...
I beg Your forgiveness and won't explain why.

Please, just forgive me! Please, just once more.
I'll make no more promises like I did before.

As I wept in sorrow, peace did enfold,
He wrapped around my spirit and comforted my soul.

His voice soft as breezes in springtime I heard—
releasing my heart like a caged wounded bird.

With instruction and warning said, "Listen to Me!"
Something essential was missing, you see.

Never in your strength can you walk along...
never in your strength will you ever be strong.

I, alone, have power over sin; I know its source
and where it will end.

Look at me always and don't turn aside.
Sin falls away as in Me you hide.

The light of My glory changes you within
destroying forever the power of this sin.

Remember this well; keep your eyes on My face,
for sin cannot enter a heart filled with grace.

Donna Shelton
2/23/93

GRACE

The wonder of grace is that it can't be earned
My love never wavers where you are concerned.

At your best or your worst all My thoughts are the same
It's with passionate longing that I speak your name.

Run, dear one, run, throw yourself on My grace
Depend on My mercy, don't turn from My face.

My arms are outstretched as I call you with love
I'll restore and refresh you with peace from above.

Donna Shelton
8/13/1997

Secret Thirteen

Praying in the Spirit

My parents were raised in churches that believed the supernatural gifts of the Spirit ceased with the last of the apostles, but something happened the year before I was born that changed everything. My grandfather was a deacon in the General Baptist Church where they believed speaking in tongues was of the devil. One Sunday, as he was at the altar praying with a young man to be saved, the Holy Spirit fell on him. He was gloriously baptized in the Spirit without even seeking it! He immediately burst forth speaking in unknown tongues at the altar of the General Baptist Church.

When the service was over, people tried to converse with him, but he would respond in tongues. He could no longer speak in English. In fact, for three days he could only speak in tongues. People thought he might have lost his mind. When he was asked questions, he could only write the answers.

As you can imagine, the General Baptists weren't pleased. The elders came to visit him and warned him that if he didn't recant this newfound experience they would have to excommunicate him from the church. What he had found was so glorious that the decision was easy for him. Because of his experience, the whole family was no longer Baptist, but Pentecostal.

Today, I think how different my life would have been if the Holy Spirit had not come uninvited to my granddad in the General Baptist Church. From an early age, I knew that speaking in tongues wasn't just a psychological phenomenon but a miraculous gift for the benefit of the Church today.

God has made a precious gift available to the believer. It's called praying in the spirit or praying in other tongues. It's impossible for me to overstate the blessing this heavenly language has been to me. What help in the secret place it is! I find the presence of God near as I pray in tongues throughout the day. I'm so thankful I was raised in a family that believed this gift of the Holy Spirit was still available for believers today.

Speaking in tongues is quite controversial in some Christian circles, but this is only because it isn't understood. Many who speak out against it do so with a bias against most other supernatural manifestations of the Holy Spirit. They say it just doesn't make sense. Of course, it doesn't make sense, because our senses only deal in the natural realm!

Christianity is a supernatural life. Many liberal theologians have even begun to deny any of the miracles of the Bible. They say the Red Sea didn't part, a fish didn't swallow Jonah, and God didn't shut the mouths of the lions for Daniel. Supposedly, these are all metaphors not miracles. What of Jesus? Was He not conceived and born of a virgin miraculously? Did He not rise from the dead? If not, Paul said our faith is futile and empty.

The entirety of our faith rests on the fact that God is a miracle-working God, and He still moves supernaturally through believers today. Praying in tongues, or what I like to call our heavenly language, belongs to this world of the supernatural. That's why it's called praying in the spirit and not praying in the mind.

As Christians, we desperately need our heavenly language to help us pray. There are so many times when we just don't know what to pray or how to pray concerning a particular issue. What are we to do if all we have available to us is our own understanding? The answer is found in the following scripture.

> Meanwhile, the moment we get tired in the waiting, God's Spirit is right alongside helping us along. If we don't know how or what to pray, it doesn't matter. He does our praying in and for us, making prayer out of our wordless sighs, our aching groans. He knows us far better than we know ourselves, knows our pregnant condition, and keeps us present before God. That's why we can be so sure that every detail in our lives of love for God is worked into something good.
>
> Romans, 8:26-28, MSG

Have you ever gotten tired in prayer because you were at a loss for words or just didn't know how to pray for a certain situation? Thank God, we're not alone in the prayer room. The Holy Spirit knows exactly what and how to pray. He knows everything about the person or situation we're lifting before the throne. He knows the will of the Father in the matter, and He's there to help us. He even takes our wordless sighs and aching groans and turns them into prayers.

> The spirit indeed is willing, but the flesh is weak.
>
> Matthew 26:41

Tiredness keeps many people from praying. If we're left with only our minds to pray, we are relying on weak flesh. The spirit is always willing, even when we're tired, so we must let our spirit take the lead.

Many mornings when I was so tired I could hardly think, I would just start praying in my heavenly language. Before long, my spirit was stirred and my mind refreshed. Then I would begin praying with my understanding.

Paul wraps this truth up well with this statement:

What is the conclusion then? I will pray with the spirit, and I will also pray with the understanding. I will sing with the spirit, and I will also sing with the understanding.

1 Corinthians 14:15

In praying for any person or situation, I will always pray with my understanding for everything I know to pray. Then I will pray in tongues. There are always things I don't know, but the Holy Spirit knows everything. As I pray in the spirit, many times I will get further wisdom from the Him on how to pray with my understanding. I will go back and forth like this until I have a sense in my spirit that the job is done.

Paul refers to worship as well when he speaks of singing with the spirit and with his understanding. Oh, what help the Holy Spirit is in worshipping this infinite God! He is beyond my understanding but as I worship in my heavenly language, the Spirit worships the Father through me. These have been some of my most glorious times in prayer. Sometimes, as I worship in the Spirit, I reach the place where words are no longer enough. I find myself with only sighs and groans. My head may not understand what they mean, but they're an expression of something coming from deep inside my heart. I'm aware that the Holy Spirit is sighing and groaning through me.

By nature I'm a skeptical person. I'm not one to accept something without investigating it first. I can relate to those who have difficulty embracing speaking in tongues or those who feel it's fine for others, but not them. First of all, I want you to know it's a gift for every believer to enjoy, so let's investigate tongues for a moment.

In 1 Corinthians 14:14, Paul said, *"For if I pray in a tongue, my spirit prays, but my understanding is unfruitful."* Praying in tongues is an activity of the spirit. When your spirit prays, you don't understand what you're saying because your head has nothing to do with it. It's a language just like English is a language, but the source is your spirit, not your head.

Years ago at the University of Pittsburgh, there was a study done on the language center of the brain. They brought in Christians who said they spoke in tongues. The scientists there wanted to see what took place in the brain when these believers spoke their so-called heavenly language. What these researchers found astonished them! While speaking in tongues, the language center of the brain was firing or working, but the rest of the brain fell silent. There was no activity whatsoever. To further test this result, researchers asked the individuals to speak meaningless gibberish that made no sense at all. Surprisingly, the whole brain fired up with activity, even though it was no language at all. They deduced from this the fact that while they were speaking in tongues there was a language being spoken, but the language center was not receiving its information from the brain. There must be another source.

With my simple mind I explain it this way: When you're speaking in English or your native language, your tongue is hooked up to your brain. But when speaking in your heavenly language, your tongue is unhooked from your brain and hooked up to your spirit. This makes complete sense to you unless you don't believe in the Spirit at all. And if you don't believe in the Holy Spirit, you can't be a Christian.

This is not to say you don't have any part to play in speaking in tongues. Acts 2:4 says, *"And they were all filled with the Holy Spirit and began to speak with other tongues, as the Spirit gave them utterance."* They *spoke*, but the Spirit gave them utterance. The Spirit gave them the language, but they had to open their mouths to speak it. One difficulty people have is that they expect the Holy Spirit to take over and do it all by Himself. But God never works this way; He works in partnership with us. He prompts, we obey.

One time, I was praying with a man who wanted to be baptized in the Holy Spirit. The Spirit came upon him in a great way and was bubbling up in him to the point where I thought he was going to burst! He was working hard to keep his mouth shut, like he was holding something from coming out of it. I tried to get him to yield to the Holy Spirit, but he just wouldn't do it. After a bit, I said, *"Why were you holding your lips so tight? Why didn't you let that language come out?"*

"Because I was afraid it would be me and not God speaking," he said.

"It *is* **you!**" I said. "God's not going to do the speaking for you. He just gives you the language, but you choose to speak it out of your mouth."

We prayed again, and this time he relaxed, opened his mouth, and spoke in his heavenly language. The issue was not about speaking in tongues but about yielding to the Holy Spirit. His resistance was not just against tongues, but against the Holy Spirit. Speaking in tongues is a gift that overflows out of our spirits when we give Him full control of our lives.

Diversity of Tongues

In 1 Corinthians 12, Paul tells us there are different kinds of tongues. The Word goes on to teach that there are four basic manifestations of tongues. It's important we know what these are and are able to distinguish each of them from the others because they each have a distinct purpose.

1. **Tongues for personal edification** (1 Corinthians 14:4). This is the supernatural language the Holy Spirit can pray through us at any time throughout the day. I call this devotional tongues.

2. **Tongues for interpretation** (1 Corinthians 14:5). This gift of tongues is accompanied by a gift of interpretation by the same or another person. The Scriptures suggests this manifestation of tongues was mainly expressed in house meetings.

3. **Tongues for intercession** (Romans 8:26). This manifestation of tongues empowers believers to intercede for their own lives, their families, their church, their city, their nation, etc. God may also use them to stand in the gap for someone or for some situation totally unknown to them.

4. **Tongues as a sign to the unbeliever** (1 Corinthians 14:22). This is the phenomenon that took place on the day of Pentecost (Acts 2:4-11). It occurs when the Holy Spirit transcends the intellect and

language barriers by empowering a believer to preach, teach, or testify about Christ in a language of men of which the believer himself has no knowledge.

Each of these manifestations of speaking in tongues is very powerful and deserves a thorough investigation, but we have only discussed them briefly for the purposes of this book. Of these four different manifestations of tongues, two are to be used in the individual prayer life of a believer: tongues for personal edification and tongues for intercession.

Tongues for Personal Edification

The focus of this book is about how we turn talking to God into walking with God. This happens as we learn and practice the truths or what I have called secrets of prayer. We can know without a doubt that God is listening.

How do we not just pray in the morning, but live in the presence of God throughout the day? One of the most helpful exercises in this great endeavor is praying in tongues for personal edification. This is the prayer language each of us receives when we're filled with the Holy Spirit. The other three manifestations of tongues are given as the Spirit wills, but this one can be engaged in any time we choose.

I pray in this personal prayer language all throughout the day, and I also encourage you to do it as often as possible. Paul said, *"I wish you all spoke with tongues"* (1 Corinthians 14:5). He goes on to say, *"I thank my God I speak with tongues more than you all"* (1 Corinthians 14:18). I'm sure there were many believers in the Corinthian church who spoke in tongues a lot, but he said you don't speak as much as I do! Obviously, Paul was not just talking about speaking in tongues only in his morning prayer. Speaking in his heavenly language continually and as much as possible was a lifestyle for Paul.

Why is it so important? Because *"he who speaks in a tongue edifices himself"* (1 Corinthians 14:4). When praying in tongues, your spiritual self is being built up, strengthened, and emboldened. Jude 1:20 says, *"But you, beloved, building yourselves up on your most holy faith, praying in the Holy Spirit.*" Praying in tongues is accomplishing something inside of you that your head knows nothing about.

Why and how does speaking in tongues edify you? Long before time began, God had a dream. That dream was you. When He dreamed of you, He laid out a perfect plan for your life. He knew everything He wanted for you and what He wanted you to do with your life. God is infinite in wisdom and knowledge. There's nothing you would ever face that He didn't know about and provide for ahead of time. He appropriated everything you would need. It's called God's providential care.

There's so much we don't know, but when God laid out this great plan for our lives, the Holy Spirit was right there with Him. He listened intently to every detail of your life as the Father planned your birth, your family, your life purpose, and every aspect of your redemption and personal life. He knows everything the Father knows. He is a co-equal with the Father and the Son. In fact, the Holy Spirit is the One who has been put in charge of overseeing God's plan for your personal life!

Then an amazing thing happened. The Holy Spirit consented to take up residence within your spirit to assist you in living out God's plan for your life. One of the main reasons He came to reside in you was to pray for you and through you. Think of that! The One who was there with the Father when He laid out His plan for your life now lives in you to assist you in working out God's plan. The Holy Spirit brought His own prayer language with Him, so He could give it to you to help you pray. When you pray in your heavenly language, it's the Holy Spirit praying through you (1 Corinthians 14:2).

When you pray or worship in tongues, the Holy Spirit is speaking through your spirit directly to the Father. Often when we pray with our understanding, we ramble on and become distracted. But every time you pray in tongues, you're assured you're speaking directly to God because the Holy Spirit is doing the praying.

Also, we speak mysteries. All that the Holy Spirit knows of the deep mysteries of God and His plan for your life is made available as you pray in the spirit. Do you see how desperately we need this prayer language? You can come up against a wall in your praying, but then switch over to your heavenly language. The Holy Spirit goes to work, praying correctly for things you don't know anything about, and the breakthrough comes.

Another benefit of tongues is that the Holy Spirit takes information, mysteries that God wants to reveal to you, and He speaks them to you. Sometimes, when praying in tongues, you're speaking to God, and at other times, God is speaking to you.

Imagine as you pray in tongues, the Holy Spirit is searching for just the right things of God that will apply to what you are praying. These are called mysteries because we don't know or understand them yet, but we will understand them later when He gives you the needed breakthrough. No eye has ever seen, nor ear heard the things that are made available to you as you pray in tongues (1 Corinthians 2:9-10). There are so many things God has prepared for us that we never tap into when we only pray with our understanding. Oh, as Paul said, I wish you all spoke with tongues!

When I face a decision, I pray everything I know to pray with my understanding. The wisdom I need doesn't always come immediately. If it doesn't, I pray in the spirit for a while and it's like a curtain is pulled back and the answer becomes clear. Why couldn't I see it before? Many times our natural mind gets in the way with questions and doubts and too many details. This only brings frustration and confusion. Praying in the spirit takes our mind out of the equation and often brings a peace that allows the answer to light up inside like a neon sign.

I may be praying for someone, but feel like I'm getting nowhere. But then, as I pray in tongues, I feel the energy of the Spirit empowering me to pray. I have a strong sense in my spirit that work is being accomplished my understanding knows nothing about. Sometimes this will lead to a heavy burden for the person falling upon me. I may begin to groan or weep with deep compassion as is spoken of in Romans 8:26. This, too, is the Holy Spirit helping me when I don't know what or how to pray.

Why did God give us such a peculiar language to use in prayer? Couldn't He just have used our earthly language to accomplish the same things? The answer is *no!* Our human language can only articulate what we know with our human understanding. There had to be a heavenly language to articulate what only heaven knows. You see, it makes perfect sense that if we are spiritual beings created in the image of God Who is Spirit, we would need a language which belongs only to the world of the Spirit. It doesn't belong to the whole spiritual world—only to the children of God. It's the language of our spiritual family.

When God's children pray in tongues, I'm sure it must drive the devil crazy. He can't understand this language. The Holy Spirit is praying divine secrets through us that will bypass all his schemes and will nullify his assignments sent against us. We must be faithful to pray much in the spirit. Oh, how much damage to Satan's kingdom and advancement of God's kingdom must be taking place while a child of God begins to pray in unknown tongues!

Strength for Any Situation

I have the strength to face any situation that comes my way because I realize where the real struggle lies...in my mind and emotions.

Sometimes it takes every ounce of my will to reign in my rampant thoughts and emotions and focus them in a positive way according to God's Word.

When they still refuse I use my secret weapon, the precious gift that Jesus left for me for just this sort of thing!

Tongues, the heavenly language that flows from the Holy Spirit in me is the one thing that stops all this nonsense in its tracks!

I pray in the spirit purposefully and intensely, knowing that what I need is being brought before the throne of grace with perfectly worded petitions.

I have no idea what is being said, but the changing tone of my yielded voice lets me know that the Holy Spirit is taking the situation in hand for me.

My spirit leaps with joy. It is done! I have no worries.

My petitions have turned to passionate praise uttered with beautiful words beyond my comprehension.

How could I ever, ever, tell my God with my puny, limited vocabulary what He means to me. Words will always fail me, but the Holy Spirit's unlimited ability won't.

Because of Him, I can pray powerful prayers, intercede with faith, and praise with abandon.

Thank You, thank You, thank You, Jesus for not leaving us powerless when You went back to the Father!

Oh, how I wish everyone who belongs to You would avail themselves of all that is theirs through the baptism of the Holy Spirit!

I for one want everything you have for me, and I don't think you will mind me being a little greedy in this one thing.

Besides, this is where the battle is always won.

Donna Shelton
1/19/04

Conclusion:

Sweet Hour of Prayer

More than forty years have past since I first entered this life of prayer. I can tell you it gets sweeter and richer as the years go by. I've spent many hours in the secret place and have experienced so many blessings I could never count them all.

There were also times where I sensed God dealing with an issue in my life. Although these days were filled with deep conviction and repentance, the judgment of God was so righteous and loving I never felt condemned. I felt secure in His loving arms. There were also days where the heavens seemed like brass, but I kept pressing on, knowing God was requiring faith and commitment to continue showing up anyway. Then, there were days where it seemed like all of heaven opened up, and I was wrapped in His holy presence. I must say, experiencing just one of those days is worth a thousand days of dryness.

There were some days where the written Word of God was the feature of the secret place. It seemed I could hear God's voice in every scripture I read. Also, there were many days where I just couldn't stop worshipping Him. It was all I could do. These days were filled with singing and tears, flowing freely as my heart was overwhelmed at the greatness and beauty of my matchless Savior. There were times when I sat in silence at His feet, being still and knowing He is God. There were moments when a deep burden for someone, a situation, our nation, or a foreign nation would fill my prayer time with intercession. I remember days sitting with a globe in my lap, weeping for His power and glory to cover the earth. There were days when my faith was challenged, and God was requiring me to step out and do something that seemed impossible. Through abiding in Him in prayer, He always made it possible!

This is the life of prayer. Every true saint who has found his or her place in God and accomplished any great work for His glory has been a person of prayer. There is no other way. We either pray or we perish. Weak Christians are weak prayers. Those who live in spiritual poverty are those who have a poor prayer life. An empty prayer room leads to an empty heart. God seeks men and women who will pray. We must never pray just to get something from God, but to get Him. Once we have Him—we have everything!

Prayer is not a duty that is fulfilled by spending time talking to God, but a life lived abiding in His Presence. If all I have said has only led you to feel obligated to fulfill a religious duty, I have not accomplished what the burden of my heart has called me to do. My desire has been to paint such a lovely picture of the secret place that you would be filled with desire to go there—to live from there.

I have never once told you that you ought, should, or better pray. If you're a true Christian, I know you want to pray. Shed any past guilt of failure in your prayer life and know that God wants to meet with you and have sweet fellowship. He is in love with you!

I urge you to begin this great journey today. Don't let anything delay you. The devil will give you every excuse imaginable why not to pray today, why not to pray right now. He will send distractions the moment you begin to go into the secret place. The devil will do everything possible to keep you out of the prayer room because he knows if you ever get there, your life will be forever changed. You are not unaware of his cunning devices, but you have the power of the Holy Spirit to help you. All you have to do is ask.

You may stumble in consistency. You may face dry days. You may not feel like you have accomplished anything on certain days. In those times, treat prayer like learning to ride a bike. If you fall, get back up and begin again. Before long, with the Holy Spirit's help, you'll be soaring in prayer. And at the end of your life, you won't regret a day spent in the secret place.

I must share in closing the story behind a hymn that is the most beautiful expression of a life of prayer that I know. This song, more than any other, speaks of the beauty of the secret place of prayer. Read each stanza carefully and reverently. They lead us to the place of prayer where this man lived in sweet communion with his God.

He was a blind preacher from England named William Wallford. A friend, Rev. Thomas Salmon, came by and Wallford asked him to write down a new poem he had composed on the subject of prayer. Three years later, Salmon showed it to the editor of the New York Observer who then printed it. Five years after that, William Bradbury set it to music. It has become a standard hymn in almost every hymnal, yet it was written about a life of private prayer.

As with him and so many other men and women of prayer, the last verse is a fitting culmination to walking with God and then being able to exchange faith for sight. May it be a theme song for all of us.

Sweet Hour of Prayer

Sweet hour of prayer! Sweet hour of prayer!
That calls me from a world of care,
And bids me at my Father's throne
Make all my wants and wishes known.

In seasons of distress and grief,
My soul has often found relief,
And oft escaped the tempter's snare,
By thy return, sweet hour of prayer!

Is God Listening?

Sweet hour of prayer! Sweet hour of prayer!
The joys I feel, the bliss I share,
Of those whose anxious spirits burn
With strong desires for thy return!
With such I hasten to the place
Where God my Savior shows His face,
And gladly take my station there,
And wait for thee, sweet hour of prayer!

Sweet hour of prayer! Sweet hour of prayer!
Thy wings shall my petition bear
To Him whose truth and faithfulness
Engage the waiting soul to bless.

And since He bids me seek His face,
Believe His Word and trust His grace,
I'll cast on Him my every care,
And wait for thee, sweet hour of prayer!

Sweet hour of prayer! Sweet hour of prayer!
May I thy consolation share,
Till, from Mount Pisgah's lofty height,
I view my home and take my flight.

This robe of flesh I'll drop, and rise
To seize the everlasting prize,
And shout, while passing through the air,
"Farewell, farewell, sweet hour of prayer!"

Rev. William W Wallford 1842
Music, William Bradbury 1861

PRAYER OF SALVATION

God loves you—no matter who you are, no matter what your past. God loves you so much that He gave His one and only begotten Son for you. The Bible tells us that "…whoever believes in him shall not perish but have eternal life" (John 3:16 NIV). Jesus laid down His life and rose again so that we could spend eternity with Him and experience His absolute best on earth. If you would like to receive Jesus into your life, say the following prayer out loud and mean it in your heart.

> *Heavenly Father, I come to you admitting that I am a sinner. Right now, I choose to turn away from sin, and I ask you to cleanse me of all unrighteousness. I believe that Your son, Jesus, died on the cross to take away my sins. I also believe that He rose again from the dead so that I might be forgiven of my sins and made righteous through faith in Him. I call upon the name of Jesus Christ to be the Savior and Lord of my life. Jesus, I choose to follow You and ask that You fill me with the power of the Holy Spirit. I declare that right now I am a child of God. I am free from sin and full of the righteousness of God. I am saved in Jesus' name. Amen.*

If you prayed this prayer to receive Jesus Christ as your Savior for the first time, please write to us to receive a free book!

www.harrisonhouse.com
Harrison House Publishers
P.O. Box 35035
Tulsa, Oklahoma 74153

The Harrison House Vision

Proclaiming the truth and the power
of the Gospel of Jesus Christ with excellence.
Challenging Christians
to live victoriously,
grow spiritually,
know God intimately.

Connect with us on

![f] Facebook @ HarrisonHousePublishers

and ![Instagram] Instagram @ HarrisonHousePublishing

so you can stay up to date with news
about our books and our authors.

Visit us at **www.harrisonhouse.com**
for a complete product listing as well as
monthly specials for wholesale distribution.